A HOLOCAUST MEMOIR OF LOVE & RESILIENCE

MAMA'S SURVIVAL FROM LITHUANIA TO AMERICA

ETTIE ZILBER

Title: A Holocaust Memoir of Love & Resilience. Mama's Survival from Lithuania to America

Author: Ettie Zilber

ISBN: 9789493056039 (ebook)

ISBN: 9789493056022 (paperback)

Publisher: Amsterdam Publishers, The Netherlands

info@amsterdampublishers.com

RECOMMENDATIONS

"Almost eight decades after the Holocaust, it is fading from memory and sometimes even unknown to younger generations - yet the details need to be maintained. Through first-person testimony and archival research, *Love and Resilience* is a formidable story of one woman's survival from Lithuania to America, told from her perspective as well as that of her Second Generation daughter. It's clear that future generations, just like this individual family, will be grateful this document exists."- **Stephen E. Herbits, former Secretary-General, World Jewish Congress**

"There has never been a more urgent need for books like Dr. Ettie Zilber's. With more and more survivors gone, the second generation must carry the twin torches of memory and of hope. This faithful, meticulous, and pure-hearted book does both."- **Sonia Taitz, author of The Watchmaker's Daughter and Great with Child**

"A Holocaust Memoir of Love and Resilience is an utterly compelling contribution to Holocaust literature. In these pages, we are privy to crucial, daily triumphs and desolation of Jewish life in Lithuania both before and during the Holocaust through the vivid and haunting recollections of Dr. Zilber's mother. As the author revisits the geography of her parents' lives, she adds her own keen experiences and observations about the places where slaughter and survival still echo, and then the impact of the tragedies on her own life." - **Rita Gabis, author of A Guest at the Shooter's Banquet: My Grandfather and the SS, My Jewish Family, A Search for the Truth**

In Memoriam

To Papa, Liova (Louis) Sidrer, who died too young, without telling
his full story
To Mama, Zlata (Lottie) Santocki Sidrer, who made sure she did
To those who didn't survive, whose stories were tragically cut short;
and to those who did, and are now gone –
you are not forgotten

Dedication

To my children and my grandchildren
You are our legacy
Know from whence you came!

Acknowledgements

To my two wonderful sisters:
Jeanne, for your love, wise counsel and for conducting and
recording the many hours of interviews with Mama; and to Rena,
for your love, support, and sharp wit;
And, to you both, for taking such loving care of Mama when I could
not be there.
To my aunt, Reva Sidrer; your sharp memory helped fill in the gaps
To my husband, Yakov, for your love and encouragement of this
project.
To the many Educational Centers, Holocaust Survivor and Second
Generation organizations, for your continuous efforts in ensuring
that the Holocaust stories are told.

CONTENTS

PART I

MAMA'S MEMOIR

INTRODUCTION

I recall my visit to Landsberg am Lech, a lovely city southwest of Munich, Germany. During the Second World War a section of the city was designated as a concentration camp; after the war it was converted into a Displaced Persons (DP) Camp in the American Zone. It felt strange wandering around the buildings where my family had lived among so many surviving refugees. Each one was trying to begin the reconstruction of their life after the horrific genocide. Many babies were born here; I was one.

I was on a mission to document the history of a woman for whom I have consummate respect and of whom I have always been in awe —my mother: a survivor of the horrors of the Holocaust, a relocated, renovated and recreated refugee who raised herself out of the ashes, like the proverbial phoenix, to establish a new life, a new future and a new dynasty, without being destroyed by the nightmares of the past. Mama's strength, resilience and unconditional love made me who I am today.

From the moment of my birth I was suckled at my mother's breast with the milk she was proud to be able to feed me; she was actually incredulous that she could give birth and nurse a child after all those dreadful years. She was so happy to have a sign of life and normalcy—a baby—after so much horror and death. But this baby digested more than milk. I absorbed my mother's stories, as well as her silent sentiments and emotions. Interestingly, today, some scientists claim that trauma changes a person's DNA, and that these genes are passed on to the following generations. All I know is that, given the carnage, I likely should never have even been born to tell these stories.

My sisters and I realized that we missed the boat in getting Papa's full story recorded before his early death from cancer at only 66 years of age. Thus, we were determined not to miss the opportunity to document Mama's voice and memory. With a sense of urgency, we decided that we would not wait any longer to record her stories. Thus, a joint effort ensued. My sister, Jeanne, interviewed Mama and recorded her responses onto CDs. Of course, Mama also told us all she knew about Papa's biography.

I received the CDs and transcribed them word for word. We encouraged Mama to express the memories of her feelings and thoughts during historical junctures and events. Once done, I had her edit and clarify the transcript. She wanted me to correct her grammar, but in truth I minimized my edits on her sentence structure and vocabulary; I wanted to ensure her own voice came through.

I also had to establish the timeline, because, as we learned from our childhood, we never heard the stories chronologically; they just popped out spontaneously and never in a linear fashion. I then embarked on verifying dates, geographic locations and events from published resources and testimonies of other survivors. Additional historical notes and references were added to corroborate or, in rare instances, to adjust her memory. Interviews with Mama and Papa from my previous genealogical research were added.

My parents did not focus their lives around their traumatic history, as did some survivors, nor did they, like others, avoid the topic altogether. Their stories were told on occasions when they fitted into the context of a conversation or when we asked direct questions. They were never recounted formally nor in order, and therefore always seemed disjointed in our minds. We were always aware that they had a normal life "*farehn krieg*" (before the war), that something terrible happened to them during "*dem krieg*" but that they survived, and the time after the war was hence referred to as "*nochen krieg*" (after the war). The horrible years were referred to as "*dem fier*" (the fire). And it was "a fire." There were approximately 210,000 Jews in Lithuania on the eve of the war. Kovno (Lithuanian: Kaunas) was a vibrant city of 35,000-40,000 Jews. Only 6,100 were left at the time of the liquidation of the ghetto in July, 1944. In total, 95% of Lithuanian Jews were killed from 1941-1945.

Given the devastation they experienced, my parents' stories were always tinged with sadness and grief, but there was also satire and, sometimes, even humor and irony. Feats of courage, pluck and *chutzpah* (cheekiness) facing the Lithuanian, Russian or German authorities were always acknowledged and recounted as if there was a moral lurking therein from which we must learn for the future—and there probably was! The stories were legion. We heard about how my grandfather cheated imminent death in the Seventh Fort by bragging about his Lithuanian military medal, how they hid money inside the smelly latrine, how they were married in a forbidden ceremony in the ghetto right before it was liquidated. There were stories about how the family established a "whistle" during the ghetto years as a warning code, how they hid the children during the *Aktsias* (roundups), and how Papa managed to escape the ghetto. There were also the stories about how Mama was responsible for registering her own mother and sisters when they arrived at the Stutthof concentration camp, about survival on the death march, and her harrowing travels after liberation back into Lithuania, which was in the Soviet sector, in order to find Papa in Kovno (just one day before his planned escape), their dangerous escape from East to West and, ultimately, the reunification of the family at the Displaced Persons camp in Landsberg, Germany.

Mama was always reluctant to share her stories publicly, unlike many others who agreed to be interviewed and videotaped by historical research organizations. She never felt comfortable going public with her war stories. She always told us about her experiences in her own way, privately, often while we were sitting in the kitchen, watching her cook or riding with her in the car. The stories would just pop out at strange times almost as if on cue, but always in context. Or we would overhear morsels of our parents' Yiddish conversations when they met up with the other *Griners* ('green' newcomers from Europe) at a dinner, holiday, or vacation in the Catskills or at Coney Island. She wanted us to know. And, yes, Mama made sure we were fluent in Yiddish.

In her later years, Mama agreed to give speeches at Lithuanian Association ceremonies and interviews with high school students. At one time, Mama was asked to do a presentation about her Holocaust experiences to members of her senior resident community in Israel. With trepidation, she agreed, but decided to focus on the "luck and coincidence" stories, rather than the horrors. She chose to tell many of the above-mentioned stories and even added a few new ones, like how a 90-year-old woman in Israel remembered *Yankefke* (Mama's father who died in Dachau) coming for Shabbat meals during the time when he was a soldier in the Lithuanian army, and how Rabbi Oshry, who married Mama and Papa, coincidentally shocked a few of our family members in the audience in South Africa after he described this forbidden wedding that he performed in the Kovno Ghetto. Such stories could fill a book, and, indeed, they all appear in this memoir, including others.

For Second Generation (2G) kids like us, one of our major difficulties was trying to understand how people found each other after the war. We could not comprehend that an entire continent was in upheaval, millions were displaced, and during a time before modern technology, how they set out to find each other. For Mama after the war, this started with a little note on a scrap of paper posted on a public bulletin board, and a coincidental meeting with her father-in-law—involving a horse and carriage, a cigarette, and the desperate search for a match. These disparate events ultimately led to the reunification of the family's survivors and, really, everything that came thereafter.

Needless to say, every survivor has innumerable and incredible stories. Many accounts have been written and published by survivors and historians over the last few decades. In addition, screen and text documentation has saved the testimonies of the remaining survivors. Like *The Ancient Mariner* by Coleridge, there is now a human imperative which drives both the survivors to tell, and the students to listen, because we know that time is running out. The living witnesses are passing on and the stories, if not documented, will disappear.

This account of my mother's (and father's) story is an attempt to add to the documentation of survivors' narratives. This narrative will ensure that her descendants will know about her family members, her history, her indomitable spirit, her courage, determination, and pluck, and her ability to move forward and live a productive and fruitful life despite the traumas. It is an attempt to comprehend the incomprehensible—the horrors of history's largest act of genocide, and of inhumanity itself. Almost as important, it is an act of defiance against the revisionists and Holocaust deniers who shamelessly defile the memories of all those millions who were killed, and the surviving souls who experienced indescribable torture and abuse.

Many friends and relatives returned to the lands of the horror and pain. Some went for soul searching and remembrance, a few as witnesses in trials, others for business and yet others for holidays and sightseeing—but not Mama. She would not ever entertain the idea of visiting Lithuania, Poland or Germany. She would even get angry at my father who traveled to Germany for work; she could not understand why he had a nonchalant attitude towards Germany, while she still felt pain and anger. She finally learned to accept the chasm of differences between their war experiences, and the resultant painful ironies: she lost almost everyone; he lost no one. She suffered extended horrors in the concentration camp and death march until her liberation in March 1945, while he escaped from the ghetto in June 1944 and was liberated by the Soviets in August 1944.

I know that it upset her every time I flew to or through Germany, or with their national carrier. And I know that she would probably be turning in her grave to know that I even travelled to Lithuania and Poland to retrace her footsteps and research Mama and Papa's European lives—75 years later.

One of Mama's imperatives was to ensure an individually marked gravesite with a tombstone so that the family could congregate annually or whenever they felt the need. Clearly, there was a deep scar in her heart as she was robbed of that consolation for her grief and loss. For this reason, she was determined to relocate, reunite and reinter Papa's remains from New Jersey to Israel—despite the complicated bureaucracy and great expense. She bought a double plot, joining him 26 years later. And Mama got her wish—this double gravesite has become our family's place of *Yorzeit* (annual memorial), grieving and updates. That's the power of Mama's love and strength.

As her daughters, the Second Generation, we felt the imperative to inform ourselves, our children—and now our grandchildren—about the family history. Dr. Elchanan Elkes, the head of the Jewish Council in the Kovno ghetto, wrote a letter to his children in England on October 19, 1943 admonishing them to "Remember ... what Amalek did to us ... Remember this and do not forget it all the days of your lives. Pass it on as a holy testament to the generations to come."[1] Mama agreed. She believed survivors must tell their stories so that the descendants and the world will know and that this history will never be forgotten.

Mama died April 2, 2015 at the age of 90. Mama, we miss you and we will not forget. So here is Mama's story, as she told us.

1. Littman, S., p. 182.

PRE-WAR LIFE IN KOVNO

I was born in Pren [Prienai], Lithuania, a small town near Kovno [Kaunas], Lithuania on February 5, 1925, to Eta [née Zivov] and Yankel [Jakob] Santocki [Yiddish pronunciation – santotsky]. [1] They were young people who ran away from home to get married [in Prienai, 1923]. Her parents were not happy about her marriage to Yankel because they thought he lacked ambition. This was what my mother told me.

My father, Yankel, was born [in Kalvarija] during Hanukah in 1903; my mother, Eta, was born in Prienai in 1905.[2] I am not sure how my father got the name Santockis which was not a Jewish one; there was a general named Santockis in Lithuanian history. I was named Zlata, possibly after Yankel's mother, Zlata Khlebowitz. Zlata means "gold" in Polish ... but nobody ever called me Goldele; can you picture me as a Goldele?

One month after my birth, my parents moved to Kovno, as the Jewish residents called Kaunas. I was the oldest of their four daughters: Ida was born on September 2, 1927; Nechama was born on May 29, 1929; and Genya was born on January 15, 1933.

My sister, Ida [her official name was Fruma]—what a girl! She was tall, beautiful, big but clumsy. She had teeth to die for. She used to stand in front of the mirror and polish them. I always envied her teeth because I had ugly teeth. She was a bright girl, full and heavy, never thin and always busy with boyfriends. They were always older than my boyfriends and she was almost two years younger than I. She sang beautifully. She read books. She and I were in the same Gymnasium #3 [high school] because she was only one year and seven months younger than I. I used to complain because she never wanted to participate in household chores, like cleaning the house. I would yell at her, saying: "What will you do when you get out of the house—you do not know how to sweep a floor." And she would answer: "When I will need to know, I will know."

My sister, Nechama, was 10 when the war began. She was really just a child in the ghetto. Her best friend was Reva Sidrer. They went to school together. They both had boyfriends whom they keep in touch with to this day. She and Reva used to spend hours observing us, their older siblings in the ghetto, as we were flirting.

I can't remember the month, but my mother was exactly 20 years older than I. She was a strong woman, really. She kept us all together. I never saw her cry, never—or complain. She just watched over us like a mother hen so everything should be just right. She did not mind a lot of crazy things, like hiding guns in the ghetto, but my father was different; he would never agree to such risks—never. During the ghetto years, we kept all secrets from him, but my mother knew all our secrets. Once, we even hid a partisan [Resistance fighter] in our basement for a while. My father never knew.

We lived in Kovno all those years, at first near the train station. Then, in 1933, we moved to a section of town called Zaliakalnis in Lithuanian, but referred to as *Auf dem Grinem Barg* [Yiddish: on the green hill] by the Jewish residents. We lived in a one-family house and on the left side a store was attached, which my parents made into a non-kosher butcher shop. This shop was their livelihood; we were not rich, but we had a comfortable life. They made a good living, had a nice house on *dem Grinem Barg*, with running water and faucets. Our address was Kapsugatwe 33 and it was not far from the beautiful boulevard, Laisves Aleja.[3]

I went to the public Lithuanian Gymnasium #3 [high school] even though most of the Jewish children of Kovno went to private Hebrew, Yiddish and religious schools, which separated boys and girls. I was one of only approximately three to ten Jews who were accepted to the public Lithuanian school. Since I wanted to become a doctor we felt that I would have a better chance of getting into medical school if I graduated with high grades from a Lithuanian public school rather than from a Jewish private school. To get into a Lithuanian university was not easy for Jews; many Jewish students had to leave Lithuania to go to England or Italy to become professionals.

No one at school knew that I was Jewish; my Lithuanian language was without an accent and my name was Lithuanian. The principal of my high school was shocked to learn that I was Jewish. There was one teacher in my school, Mr. [Boris] Shulgasser, who was also Jewish. He taught German. He was actually a childhood classmate of my father's [from Kalvarija]. He recognized my name at roll call. In later years in the ghetto my mother gave him food because he was starving.[4]

I was a good student and I was fluent in Lithuanian—always getting the top grade of five in Lithuanian language, however, I did not do that well in Chemistry. My Lithuanian was so good that I actually tutored a Lithuanian classmate in his language and he helped me with Chemistry.

I recall the wonderful opportunity I had received to learn about opera. I had a Russian neighbor, who was a musician. He had a daughter my age and he wanted her to learn about opera. She did not want to go to the opera so he would invite me to join them so that she would agree to attend. I did not know anything about opera but I learned a lot by the exposure I received—and with the taste came the knowledge. I saw every opera except *La Traviata*. I was always very thankful to her father for that. It was a big treat to be able to go to the beautiful opera house in Kovno and sit in the president's loge. I was even allowed to leave school in the middle of the school day to watch the best rehearsals. We got special permission from the principal of the school because they wanted us to be cultured.

We had dances every Saturday night, and I had a nice and normal life. I did not go out with *goyim* [non-Jewish boys]; my father forbade it. So, I went to the Hebrew school gatherings and I met my first love, Sia Feinzohn. He and his family came from Riga, Latvia. He lived with his mother and sister, as his father had died. They spoke mostly German at home and were not able to speak Lithuanian well, so we used to laugh at them because their accents sounded funny to us. Nevertheless, he and I could communicate well together because I spoke Yiddish and he spoke German and these two languages are similar; we got along very well … until the end when he was killed in the massacre at the Seventh Fort.

I actually met Papa [Liova Sidrer], who would later become my husband, before the ghetto period. It was during the time that the Russians were in Kovno, around 1940. He used to appear at the ice skating rink in the winter. I did not care for him much at that time because he used to trip me on the ice. In those years he lived with his family in Slabodka [Viliampole]. They lived in an apartment above their large metal foundry.[5] He attended the Yiddish school, Shalom Aleichem [previously known as Comertz Gymnasium]. After the Russians [nationalized the factory and] evicted them from their home, they moved two blocks away from where we lived. His mother used to come to our butcher shop to buy meat, so my parents knew her.

---

1. Zlata and the spellings and pronunciation of her family name: Mama's Yiddish spelling of her family name was Santocki (or sometimes with a –y), but, pronounced phonetically as – Santotsky. Lithuanian family names for men ended in '–is', thus, Yakov spelled his name Santockis. Family names for married women ended in '–iene', thus Eta was Santockiene, as she signed on

official documents. Similarly, family name for unmarried women ended in –yte, thus Zlata was Santockyte, as was spelled on her school documents.

2. Yankel's Dachau death certificate indicates a birthdate of March 5, 1901. He might have changed his year of birth to make him seem younger and more "fit" for work. The same is true for Eta, whose Stutthof camp registration document indicates that she was born in 1906.

3. Kaunas Archives, Floor Plans (1931). Mr. Sokolovich, the owner of the house at Kapsugatwe 33, requested a permit to renovate this wooden house. Thus, the house was not owned by the Santocki family and most likely was rented.

4. Boris Shulgasser survived the war and immigrated to Mexico, where he was head of a Jewish school in Mexico City.

5. Baran, R. (2017). After the Soviet invasion, the family was evicted from this home and the factory was confiscated. They also feared that they would be sent to Siberia.

WAR: RUSSIANS, LITHUANIANS & GERMANS

All that was before the war broke out. Meeting no resistance, the Russians occupied [annexed] Lithuania in June 1940. They were followed one year later by the Germans in June 1941; life changed immediately.

When the bombing began, our normalcy disappeared. I distinctly remember the day the war began. It was a Saturday evening, June 21, 1941. I was only 16, that's right, and my boyfriend, Sia Feinzohn, had just brought me home after an evening of dancing in a park where young people went to dance every Saturday. As we stood talking in front of my house, we heard bombs. Very little did we understand what was happening at that moment, really. The Germans were bombing the airport; we had a small airport in Aleksotas, that's the name of that area outside of Kovno.

My mother, like all mothers, was waiting for her daughter to come home from the date. "Come into the house. Fast," she said. Sia went home and I went into the house. That's when I learned that our war had begun and that the Germans were bombing the small airport in Aleksotas outside the city. I do not recall if I realized at that moment that our lives would never be the same.

So, how do you go about dealing with a war? What do you do? My parents said: "We're leaving. We are going by foot towards Russia." My mother began packing things for our escape. I can still see it now, she packed a bag full of dried breads; somehow, it was as if she had prepared and collected it in advance. We did not leave immediately on the Sunday morning because we were waiting for Sia to join us, as he promised. But he never arrived, so we set out without him.

We had one bicycle onto which we loaded whatever we could carry from the house. All four children, my mother and my father started walking in the direction of Russia. We were going from Kovno toward Shavl [Siauliai, about 130 kilometers from Kaunas], north of the city. We thought to get away from the direction of the Germans; we were trying to reach the Russian border—at least that was our aim, but we were not the only ones. Hundreds and hundreds of people were on the roads. The Russian military was also trying to escape towards Russia.

We walked for days and nights, trying to move forward daily and trying to sleep on roadsides or in the fields. I don't remember how many days we walked, must have been five or six. I remember being hungry and picking strawberries in the field, which we ate with the dry bread. I always liked it. We got water from the farmers along the way.

Suddenly we heard airplanes approaching and we jumped into the ditches at the side of the road, the soldiers and us too. The planes were aiming and shooting at us. This was the first time in my life that I saw dead people lying on the side of the roads.

We thought we were going in a direction away from the Germans but we were way before Shavl [Siauliai] and the Germans were already there. We were forced to turn back to Kovno. When we returned to the city, the Germans were already in town and as soon as we marched in they arrested us and brought us all to the Seventh Fort. They took away the men and women separately.

The new reality of our lives became dramatically evident when we saw that the armed guards were not Germans, but rather Lithuanians.[1] As a matter of fact, I recognized a schoolmate of mine who was standing on one of the hills surrounding the fort. He held a rifle and was guarding us. Funny, I used to tutor him in Lithuanian grammar. Imagine, he was a Lithuanian who did not know his own language well and suddenly here he was standing with a rifle over me. Seeing him was my first shock of realization of our situation. Interesting, today I don't remember any of my teachers or school-mates; I have erased anything that has to do with Lithuania and Lithuanians from my mind. I do not want to know about it. I have even forgotten the language which I knew so well and even tutored Lithuanians in.

It was a difficult time; we were hungry and dirty and all we had to eat was stale green bread. The men were completely separated from us in a different field. The women huddled together in bunkers. At night, the guards came to look for girls. So my mother and younger sisters lay down on top of me so I was safe. Luckily, this trick worked and I escaped almost certain rape.[2]

Groups of men were marched into the Seventh Fort each day; we stood and watched them pass by us. In one of the groups I saw my boyfriend Sia and he saw me too. He was caught and kept in the prison. So I went to find my Lithuanian classmate, the guard with the gun. I called to him and he came down to speak to me. "You must do me a favor and take me to the men." He said that he would call me when the time was right. It took a day or two and he found me and I followed him first around and then inside the fort; it was a tremendous place. I saw all the men sitting on the ground. I remember this as if it were yesterday, I swear to God. I also wanted to find my father. I didn't think I would be able to find him among so many people, but suddenly, I saw him; he was actually sitting quite close to the entrance from the field.

I asked my classmate, the guard with the rifle, to find my boyfriend, Sia. He asked for his name and had him paged over a loudspeaker.

Sia came over and told me the story of how he was arrested: "I was on my way to meet you with your family but I was caught and arrested." It had been over two weeks ago. I showed him where my father and my mother's cousin were seated. "Go and stay with them, so at least you will be together," I told him.

Before I left, he said: "Probably the men will not get out of here, but the women they will let go. Please find my mother and sister and say goodbye for me; please take care of them." I left them with tears and a heavy heart, wondering if I would ever see him or my father again. That night we heard shooting; it continued all night long without end.[3] We knew they were killing all the men. My mother hugged and held us closely together and all we could do was cry.

All the women were [then] taken to the Ninth Fort, which was closer to the town of Slabodka [Viliampole]. I don't know how many days we were kept there, but eventually we were released. My mother and the four of us suddenly found ourselves standing outside the fort—out in the middle of nowhere, not knowing where we are and standing and thinking what to do. I asked my mother: "How will we get back home without our father? How are we going to live?" We were all sure that our father was dead. My mother was a strong woman and she answered me straight: "Don't worry, we will find our home; as long as I have this little coat we will be okay; we will have food." She was referring to my little sister's coat, which she had been carrying personally since we left our home; she never let it out of her hands. I later learned that it had twelve gold coins sewn inside instead of buttons. It did help us a lot eventually.

I also found out that when we were trying to run away, she was wearing a pair of shoes with heels. She never took off her shoes. It turned out that inside the shoes she had paper money hidden. Because she wore the shoes so long and walked a lot, the money moved, the shoes had nails and the nails had cut into the money. In the ghetto, she took it all out; it was foreign money from South Africa inside the lining of the shoes. We used the gold coins as well as the paper money, so we didn't suffer as much as others. We had to sell the money for less because it had holes in it because of the nails in the shoes.

We walked to a main road and asked someone where this road led. They told us it leads to Slabodka; once we had our bearings we knew how to get home. It took us a full day, from morning to night, even though it was not so terribly far. We walked through Kovno, up to *Auf dem Grinen Barg* and we came back to the home which we had left over two weeks before. I think that my mother had taken and kept the keys with her. We opened the door, and when we entered, we saw that the house was empty except for furniture. We slept that first night back in our home again.

Seeing lights in our house, a neighbor of ours, who happened to be a Russian, came over and found us back in our home. He told us that he took everything that was movable out of our house and he hid it. He said that he overhead neighbors saying: "They are not going to come back so let's go in and take their things. If they return, we will give it back to them, and if not..."

Now, we were not the richest people in town, but we were well to do by comparison to others. For example, my mother had a fur coat and nice clothes. He returned many of our possessions; there were quite a few things we could use to barter and continue to live off.

So, here we were at home. We were sure that all the men were killed and we had to get used to the fact that Papa was not coming back. I don't remember the exact time—maybe it was a few weeks later—when a woman came running to tell my mother that she saw her husband—our father—in a group of men who were being taken from one place to another, passing by a specific corner of the city. My mother found out on which corner he would be passing and she and I went to wait there. She saw him and he saw us, as he walked by with ten other men. My mother almost fainted; now we knew he was alive and he knew that we were alive. We couldn't stop crying from happiness. We didn't know where they were taking them every day.

One day Papa suddenly appeared in the doorway of our home. Seeing him was indescribable. He told us what had happened to him and how he survived the killings and how he came home that night. We had heard the shooting and about the horrible massacres that took place at the Seventh Fort. He then described what he had seen and experienced. They took groups of eight or ten men and told them to dig a big pit and take off their boots and shoes; they then were shot and fell into the grave. Thousands were killed this way.

Papa described what happened when it was his turn to be taken to be shot. He had already dug the pit and he had to remove his boots. His feet had swollen and he was having difficulty taking them off. At this moment he casually commented to one of the guards: "I want you to know that you are about to shoot a *Savanoris*." [The *Savanoris* were decorated freedom fighters who had volunteered to fight for Lithuania in their war of independence from Kaiser Germany.][4] As the story goes, they were outmanned and outgunned and were considered real heroes in Lithuania. It was a great honor to be a *Savanoris* in Lithuania and he always carried his medal with him. He even had his medal in his pocket at that very moment and showed it to the guard as proof of his status.

My father used to love to tell us about his army experiences as a *Savanoris*. As a proud *Savanoris*, my father always bragged about being invited to the presidential celebrations on Lithuanian Independence Day and marching in the parades. He would tell us funny anecdotes about how he drank milk directly from a cow's udder when the troops passed through local villages. He also told us about how the Jewish soldiers were allowed to leave ranks for Shabbat meals, which were hosted by Jewish families in the *shtetls* [small villages].

Coincidentally, it was 50 years later when I met the 90-year-old aunt of my friend Chaviva, who was visiting from Kovno. The aunt started telling me that she was from a small *shtetl* [village] in Lithuania. I had heard of the region from my father's stories when he was a soldier in the Lithuanian army. I recounted his story about how, as a soldier, he used to be invited to a Jewish home for a Shabbat meal. He told me about this experience and that this family had two young daughters. He enjoyed these visits. Suddenly, the old aunt jumped up and asked: "*Yankefke?*" Indeed, she was one of the young daughters in this family and remembered him by the nickname the family gave him. She remembered that he had a great sense of humor and told them lots of jokes. From then on she referred to me as *Yankefke*'s daughter. I enjoyed listening to her memories of my father during his young soldier years.

Well, the Lithuanian guard was impressed and said: "Okay, take your boots and come with me."[5] He walked him back to the prison. As they were walking, my father saw a friend and told the guard that he was also a *Savanoris*. The guard allowed the friend to join them. They were taken to a shack where there were three more men. The guard told them not to move until further notice. From this shack they were transferred to the Kovno prison. That was how he survived the massacre of the Seventh Fort. Nevertheless, he was still beaten and his ribs were injured. This gave him pneumonia. He put compresses on his wounds but he was very sick with fever.

While Papa was in prison the Germans took a group of men to work in the Gestapo building [on Gastucho Gatwe]. This was a big beautiful building not too far away from the prison. They had to clean the floors, the kitchen and wash the toilets. One day, while he was washing the kitchen, he saw that they were preparing chickens. He turned to the German officer who was in charge of the kitchen and told him that he was an experienced butcher: "I can take care of the chickens for you." The officer agreed, but my father added: "But I am not clean enough to work with food. Let me go home, wash and change and I will come back in the morning." So they escorted him home that evening, to our great surprise and exhilaration. At home, he bathed and changed clothes but he was sick with pneumonia. He told us that he was hit in the ribs with the butt of a rifle, which caused the illness. He never told the Germans how sick he was.

The next morning a German guard came to pick him up and escort him back to work. He continued working even when he got very sick with typhus, during the big ghetto epidemic—but the doctors wouldn't name it. We brought Dr. Berman to the house to help him and we all nursed him through this illness. Even the Germans came to check on him to see if he was really sick or not; needless to say, we were very worried when we saw the Germans come into our home. He never told them that he had typhus. This job saved his life and ours because we always had food even during the difficult ghetto years. My father worked in the Gestapo kitchen for almost three years until they liquidated the ghetto and everything went *kaput*.

I remember hearing that my father had a friend who was in the Gestapo prison building where my father was working. This man gave my father quite a bit of money through the bars of the cell to give to his family in the ghetto because he was afraid that he would never get out. My father was such a good man, he gave the family the money—that was my father—such an honest man. He told the family that he saw their father in the prison.[6]

---

1. Zlata's account is supported by Mishell, W.W. p. 391, who writes about the Lithuanian Activist Front (LAF), young Lithuanians who wore white armbands and murdered thousands of Jews. Baran, R. (2017) also recalls the German bombing of the airport and immediately seeing Lithuanians with white armbands removing arms and ammunition out of the apartment building opposite their home on Kalnyechu Gatwe 15.
2. See Petrikenas, V. & Kosas, M.; Association of Lithuanian Jews in Israel; *Holocaust Atlas of Lithuania*; Rassen, J.; and Gens, A.U. for more details and accounts of the killings, rapes and abuses at the Seventh Fort and the 70 *Savanoris* who were spared from these killings.
3. Petrikenas, V. & Kosas, M., pp. 132-3, state that "A total of 2,500–3,000 Jews were shot to death at the Seventh Fort. Other sources estimate the number of victims as 5,000. The shootings were carried out by Rollkommando Hamann, 1st Battalion, 3rd Unit, Sonderkommando 1b, and Einsatzkommando 3." Yad Vashem research estimates 6,000 to 7,000 were killed at the Seventh Fort (USHMM, p. 242).
4. Levin, D., p. 117: "Between 1918-1923, 3,000 Jews served in the military; On December 29, 1918, the government issued a call for volunteers to defend

the country against invasion, publishing its declaration in 4 languages, including Yiddish. Over 500 Jews joined the 10,000 or so volunteers who signed up ... 23 Jewish soldiers were awarded Lithuania's highest medal, The Vytis Cross, for bravery in battle, and at least 73 were killed in the fighting."

5. *Holocaust Atlas of Lithuania*: "Some 70 men survived because they had fought as volunteers in Lithuania's wars of independence in 1918-1920."

6. See Gempel. Mama didn't know that the person she described in the Gestapo prison was Berel Gempel, a fellow butcher and prisoner. He thought he would be killed and gave Yakov Santocki gold coins to give to his brother, Leib, in the ghetto. The story and name were revealed in Gempel's testimony. Indeed, Yakov was honest and delivered the coins to the brother. Gempel survived the war but his brother did not. Gempel, his wife, Zlata and Liova escaped Kovno together as described in this memoir. They all remained close friends for many years.

LIFE IN THE KOVNO GHETTO

As of August 1941, according to German decree, we had to start wearing the yellow Star of David on our clothes. And by mid-August of 1941, the 30,027 remaining Jews were ordered to relocate to the ghetto which was created out of the poor neighborhood of Slabodka [Viliampole].[1]

It is difficult to describe how so many people had to suddenly move out of their homes to another place. Everyone had to fend for themselves. I do not know how my parents arranged the details but I remember that we hired a big horse and carriage—not a modern one—and took with us whatever we could. We had to leave a lot of things behind, so my mother gave away the crystal, silver, chandeliers, some furniture, beds and linens to our neighbor. We took my father out on a mattress on this carriage because he could hardly move; he was still very sick with pneumonia. He was sick for a long, long time. He was so sick that we brought Dr. Berman, the best doctor in Kovno, to treat him. We walked alongside the carriage.

We got a tiny two-room house on the border of the ghetto. These living spaces were distributed by the Ghetto Committee in collaboration with the police. Of course the non-Jewish Lithuanians took over our homes and lived more comfortably than ever before. This was encouraged by the new rules in the city. I don't know which Lithuanians lived in this house before us, but we eventually settled into that little two-room house; it was dark and small, but it was lovely because it was just for us and we didn't have to share it with anyone else at that time. It was wonderful simply because we were all together; it was so important for us to be together. We later moved from this house after the big *Aktsia* [round up].

Mama always used to cook and sew. We needed new clothes so she used to sit with Mrs. Sidrer, my future mother-in-law, and chat and sew. Once, my friends snuck a chicken into the ghetto, killed it and gave it to my mother and said: "You cook it and we will come to eat." My mother made soup and we all enjoyed it.

My father continued working in the Gestapo kitchen like he started when he got out of the Seventh Fort. Every morning he would be picked up and he was brought back by guards late at night. They wanted him to be clean because he was working with their food. He was sick for a long time but he hid his illness from the Germans. Amazing. Somehow, we managed through the ghetto years. Because of his job, Papa was allowed to take home the *fligalach* and *heldzalach* [wings and necks] of the chickens. We were lucky to have this advantage. My mother cooked them and made soup and also fed a lot of other people too. I remember that she fed my high school German teacher [Mr. Shulgasser]. He was so embarrassed to have to ask for handouts, so my mother sent us out of the house.

Not long after we moved into the ghetto, the first *Aktsia* took place on August 18, 1941. They took 500 of the elite members of the Jewish community, including doctors, lawyers, engineers, etc. and killed them right away; they never came back. This was known as the "first *Aktsia*." These were the first to go.[2]

I recall a time when we ran out of wood and it was a typically cold Lithuanian winter. We had a wood-burning stove. We had no gas to cook on in those days. There were a lot of shacks, gates, fences made of wood. Everyone was trying to scavenge for wood. We once went and took apart a whole house, like a log cabin, with many pieces of wood; we took it apart and *shlepped* [carried] it home and chopped it up for firewood. I think I went with Ida and I recall that my little sister, Nechama, injured her finger from the saw and had a piece of her finger missing.[3]

Since I was only 17, I was too young to work, but I did anyway and went to work in place of my mother, using her name. Eventually, I got another job. I would leave early in the morning before sunrise with a brigade of men and women *afen aerodrome* [at the airfield]. It was located approximately 10 kilometers outside Kovno. The Germans were building a new airport and our brigade worked there clearing and shoveling the area for construction work. We worked from sun up to sun down. We were forced laborers. I think Sunday was off, if I remember correctly. The aerodrome of Aleksotas was completed in 1942.

I just remembered a job opportunity I was given in the ghetto. Since my father worked for the Gestapo kitchen, my father took me to work there, too. My job was to clean the floors and the carpets. I had to shake out the carpets through the back window. The back of the kitchen faced my high school courtyard and the Lithuanian kids were out playing during recess. I got so angry I closed the window and refused to go back to work there. Imagine, I gave up a comfortable job because I couldn't stand seeing these kids; it hurt me so much to see the kids playing sports and I was washing floors. I can still see it; I cried like a baby. I said: "I don't want to see them."

Also, a huge building was constructed in the ghetto for all the *werkstaten* [workshops]. This building had many sections with services for the Gestapo and the army. For example, there was a laundry, a section for sewing and darning socks; there were shoemakers, electricians, etc. Feival, my future father-in-law, was an electrician and he opened an electrical department in that same *werkstaten*. Liova, his son, also worked there as an electrician [for carrying out this job he was given food].[4] He used to go out and climb the electrical poles. I remember passing by and looking up at him; he was very good looking.

At one point, I switched from the aerodrome labor to work in the laundry *werkstaten* washing clothes by hand with the scrub board. My second job was ironing. This job of ironing was an education in perfection. I became an expert in ironing the white shirts for the Gestapo elite. My next job was darning socks. I loved this job the best because while darning socks, we would sit around telling stories and singing. I worked there until July 1944, which was the end of the ghetto.

At some point, the Ghetto Committee established a school for the young children. Nechama and Rivka [Reva] attended the ghetto school together; they were both 12 years old. However, the Gestapo closed it after two months.

One day, the Germans announced that everyone had to give up their money, silver, gold and any other items of value.[5] They went from house to house demanding and taking whatever they found in each house. My mother wasn't about to submit to this demand— that was my mother—and so she wrapped up all the paper money and coins and dropped it in the latrine in our outhouse. It is difficult to believe but after the Germans left, we went and pulled it out —the entire package. We washed every item and put it out on our beds to dry. Nechama, my only remaining sister, and I remember this event vividly until this very day. I remember the terrible smell when we retrieved it and uncovered the money. This money spared us from total poverty and hunger in the ghetto.

I also remember the "big *Aktsia*." It was a cold day with snow on the ground. Everyone was told to go outside to *Democratu* Square, and stand in groups according to their jobs, place of work. This started around five or six o'clock in the morning. We looked for my grandmother who was in another group, hoping to find her and get her out, but we could not find her or my father's sister. The Germans came in and started the "selection." Left and right; left and right. At least half of the people in the ghetto were killed ... thousands, families were broken up. It was the biggest tragedy; all were killed on that day; all were shot. To this day, every year on October 28 we hold a memorial ceremony. I will never forget the name of the Gestapo Sargent Rauca, who sent 10,000 Jews to their death at the Ninth Fort on that day. I want his name to be recorded here.[6]

The Germans took all of the people in this group to the small ghetto, and then they were taken to the Ninth Fort and killed. Whoever remained after this selection was allowed to go back to their houses. We remained with our nuclear family intact, but we lost my grandmother [Ester Liba Zivov] and my father's sister [Berta Blatiene] in this *Aktsia*. That's how I lost my grandmother. She was still a young woman at that time. If I was 16 and my mother was 35, then she was approximately 61.

At the end of the big *Aktsia*, my father and I stood with our family among a group of the Gestapo workers.[7] After the big *Aktsia*, when thousands of people were taken away, they made us relocate again. After only three months we had to leave our little apartment and move to another small house which had only one big room, a little kitchen and another small room. Every house had a latrine outside and there was no running water. This place was so small. But we adapted quickly to our new situation. You had to adapt or you would be lost.

Why were we given this house? We told them that we had two more people who were going to live with us. This is when we sought out Sia's mother and sister to move in with us. Why did we invite them in? Because I had promised Sia when I last saw him in the Seventh Fort that I would take care of his mother and sister. My father and I felt obliged to fulfill the promise made to a dead man. So we went to look for them, found them and took them into the apartment. So we all lived together like this through the ghetto years. I must say that this wasn't the best idea, but we had no choice. I recall that the mother was not a very nice woman; she used to steal food from my mother. Really, if she hadn't stolen, my mother would have given it to her anyway. Her daughter, Rivka, was a lovely girl, and a little older than I. They weren't very happy people.

Across the street from our home lived a very dear friend, Misha

Novick, with his family. And across from Misha lived the Sidrers—my future in-laws. They lived on Zanavicu Street. Mrs. Sidrer used to come to visit my mother often because her daughter Rivka and my sister Nechama were good friends. One day, Mrs. Sidrer, who was a good seamstress, was visiting my mother and she asked me to go across the street to her home to bring her scissors. They had a one-room apartment divided by a curtain among two or three families. I went to look for the scissors and opened the curtain to their side of the room and there he was—standing half naked bent over a basin washing himself. It was Liova. I knew who he was, as I had observed him on the streets and up on the electric poles where he worked on electrical maintenance. I took one look at him, I didn't say anything, I just grabbed the scissors and ran back home. "Mrs. Sidrer," I exclaimed, "your son has quite a body." She responded cynically: "Take it easy, take it easy, girl. Don't fall in love." I am afraid it was too late; we did fall in love.

We were a happy family as long as we were together. We used to have gatherings almost daily in this tiny house with only one and a half rooms. The Sidrers would come with Rivka. Then there were my best friends: Beba, Danke Lieberman. I am not going to name all of my boyfriends or you will think badly of me. They came to the house every single day after work. I had one girlfriend, Nechama, who was a distant relative, but the rest of my friends were all boys.

We used to drink vodka. I don't remember where we got the cheap vodka—it certainly wasn't Finlandia. My mother used to cook. We were not hungry because Papa was always able to bring food home. We had a *patifone* [record player] and played records, sang together until lights out and everyone had to go home for curfew. We used to dance. We had fun. As long as there is some food and drink, you make your own fun ... and *zehuze* [that's it]. Liova used to come to the house, too, and listen to the *patifone*.

Sundays we didn't have to work, so we used to walk around the streets of the ghetto and meet other friends. The ghetto had a good orchestra and once in a while we had concerts; this was wonderful. We had lots of friends between the ages of 17-20 and every chance we had, we would get together to listen to music and try to forget our daily problems. Once we had a big problem; my friends overstayed the curfew [9 p.m. from January to May 1942 and then 10 p.m. after May] and everyone had to stay overnight and sleep on the floor.[8]

Liova always loved to dabble with electronics. In the ghetto, he built a shortwave radio. We had to hide it but we were able to listen to the news from the BBC. It was a big risk because had anyone found out we could have been killed. Also, Liova used to receive old guns, which were smuggled into the ghetto, and fix them for our Resistance. My mother participated in hiding them. My father was a wonderful man but he was always so worried about us. He was concerned that we shouldn't make any false moves which would hurt us, [like] overstaying curfew. Luckily, he never knew about some of our activities.

One day, while we were sitting in a back corner of our small home, with a bed and a curtain to separate us from the rest of the living area, he [Liova] showed me how to load the gun; all of a sudden, the gun went off, and almost hit me in the thigh. We were sitting on the bed and the bullet went into the pillow which muffled the sound. Liova jumped up and broke a light bulb. My mother rushed in at that moment and understood what had happened. "Okay guys, just watch out." From then on we were a little more careful.

One of the many new laws in the ghetto [from July 24, 1942] was the one forbidding women to give birth under threat of death.[9] As it turned out, my mother did get pregnant. Because of the risk involved, she decided to have an abortion. I remember the doctor who came to our home. I remember that my mother did not make a sound—not a sound—during this time, and there was no anesthesia. I was there in that room with her during the abortion. This is a testament to my mother's strength and the challenges of our lives in the ghetto.

Like all Jewish communities, if there were ten people, there were eleven political parties and opinions. The ghetto was no different. There were right wingers, left wingers, middle wingers, you name it. There was Betar and then there were the leftists. We did not join anyone officially but we helped the ones in which we had friends. What was their aim? To escape from the ghetto and reach the woods to join the partisans. They had members who were very active outside the ghetto. There were those who got in touch with the partisans in the woods. It was not an easy objective. You needed ammunition, guns, clothing and a way to get there.

One of the biggest problems was to sneak boys and girls out of the ghetto in order to find ammunition and German military uniforms. The ghetto police helped a lot, but of course, everything was done late at night. Without the help from the outside, it would have been difficult. However, if there had been more help, more would have survived. Small groups were leaving the ghetto, but they decided among all the diverse political factions that they would not fight among themselves and go together. They went out [possibly to the Augustow Forest] in small groups. In the beginning it was difficult. It took a few years to get people out of the ghetto, one by one. Once the Germans captured a whole group sneaking out and took them to the Gestapo station—and from the Gestapo to the Ninth Fort and death.

A major event in the ghetto was the public hanging of Mek [November 18, 1942].[10] I remember it very well. Everyone was forced to watch as the Gestapo hung him in the central meeting square of the ghetto. There were secret photos taken of this event [by Zvi Kadushin/George Kadish]. He was hung because he tried to escape from the ghetto.

In December 1942, 16,600 Lithuanian Jews were left alive in the ghetto.[11] Between September to December 1943, there were about 60 prisoners working in the Ninth Fort. They were a combination of Jewish police, who had been arrested by the Gestapo after an *Aktsia*, plus other random detainees and some Russian soldiers.

They were forced to fulfill the most horrible job. Their job [as *Sonderkommando*] was to dig out the bodies that were buried for a long time in a mass grave, remove any gold teeth from the mouths of the dead, and burn these corpses in a big bonfire. This was a job that was unimaginable and they knew very well that once they completed their work they would be killed too. So they planned an escape.[12]

They did not tell anybody except those who could help arrange for the escape. They decided that the best time would be Christmas Eve. They collected vodka and offered it to the guards, some of whom were Lithuanian and others who were German. The guards drank so much vodka that they fell asleep. The prisoners escaped from the second or third floor of the Fort using bed sheets tied together. During the escape, they unlocked all the cells and told all the other prisoners to leave. They escaped through the front gate. The Jewish prisoners headed to the ghetto where they knew they would be protected and hidden; the rest ran to the woods. Those who ran to the woods were caught.

Liova was one of the *chevre* [member of the circle], so he knew what was happening. The night of the escape, Liova was called out to help the escapees. I remember him knocking on our window that night. I unlocked the door and he told me the story. He stank terribly. The Jewish escapees who came to the ghetto were well hidden in the *malinas* [underground bunkers] prepared by our *chevre*.

He told me that before being hidden, they were fed, washed and their clothes were burned—the stench from their clothes was awful and their bodies also smelled terribly. He said that you could not breathe. Right after they were hidden, their families and friends were notified. This event was a tremendous experience and achievement for both the prisoner-escapees and the ghetto residents.

The main objective was to deliver them to the partisans because they could not remain in the ghetto; we were sure that someone would inform the Germans. Of course, the Germans came to look for them in the ghetto but they weren't found. Eventually, they successfully reached the partisans in the woods. Miraculously, most of them survived; we met them after the war. Some remained in Kovno or Vilna and some went to Israel or North America. All were from Kovno and one of them was our good friend, Berel Gempel.

There were a few more *Aktsias*. They started emptying the ghetto, taking people to Estonia and to Latvia. Many of my friends were taken in these *Aktsias*. Beba and Danke were taken away to Shantz, which was part of Kovno; Ester and Chana were taken to Estonia. Very few of my friends were left in the ghetto. They took them first to work camps and later to the concentration camps.

The biggest *Aktsia* was the *Kinder Aktsia* [children's roundup] on March 27, 1944.[13] On that day, [after] all the people went to work [outside the ghetto] they locked up the entire ghetto; all the people went to work. They came in with trucks and took away all the children. All the mothers who would not allow their children to be taken were taken too. My little sister, Genya, and my mother were hidden together in a basement *malina* [hiding place] under our small house. This was the place where we once hid an escapee from the police. Nechama and her friend Reva, Liova's sister, were also hidden [there]. We covered it so well that no one would know there was an entrance.[14]

I recall the day of the *Kinder Aktsia* very well because they closed the ghetto and I could not go to work. So, instead I went to the Sidrers' home, as I had already begun to have a relationship with Liova at that time. I remember that the Gestapo came into the Sidrers' house looking for children. We were sitting around and on the wall was the "famous" photo of Liova as a baby sitting in his mother's lap. The Gestapo insisted on knowing where this child was. We had to convince him that the child was already an adult—and he was sitting right there in front of them. That was in March 1944 and it was the last of the *Aktsias*.

The atmosphere and morale in the ghetto was the lowest after the *Kinder Aktsia* in March of 1944. That was the big one. Everyone was demoralized and saddened. It was just thereafter, in April, when Liova and I decided to get married—just like that. Everyone thought we were crazy, but we decided to do it. So my parents set about making the arrangements.

---

1. See Elkes, J., p. 26. The order to wear the yellow Star of David was published on July 10, 1941. The Germans installed a provisional mayor for Kaunas, Kazimieras Palciauskas, who actively collaborated with the Nazis and was responsible "...for orders requiring all Jews to surrender their homes, move into the Viliampole ghetto ... wear the yellow star ... ban them from public streets from eight in the evening to six in the morning ... for collecting the valuables confiscated from Jews and turning them over to German authorities" (Mishell, W.W., p. 59 & Littman, S., p.173).

2. See Tory, A., pp. 54-55; Elkes, J., p. 28; Mishell, W.W., p. 67; Ancestry Memorial pages, and Yad Vashem Research Projects. According to some sources, murder operations against the Jews were carried out at the Fourth Fort on August 2, 1941, when 209 people were murdered, and on August 8 or 9, 1941, when more than 500 Jews were murdered. Between 534 and 711 Jewish intellectuals were shot to death at the Fourth Fort on August 18, 1941 in a so-called intelligence operation. In addition, according to German sources, approximately 1,800 Jews were shot at the Fourth Fort on that day. The shootings were carried out by members of Rollkommando Hamann, 1st Battalion, 3rd Unit and of Einsatzkommando 3 of Einsatzgruppe A.

3. USHMM, p. 244: "On January 5, 1942 German ghetto guard chief prohibits demolishing houses or parts of houses or fences. Ghetto inmates, desperate for fuel ... defy the prohibition."

4. Baran, R. (2017).

5. Tory, A., p. 34; USHMM, p. 243.

6. Gabis, R., pp. 173 & 347. SS Rottenführer Albert Helmut Rauca was the Gestapo Jewish Affairs specialist in Kovno and commander of the Kovno ghetto. For more on this horror and those that followed, see Elkes, J.; Littman, S.; Yad Vashem Research Projects; and CBC Canada.

7. Some workers deemed useful to the Germans were issued special passes, sometimes referred to as "life certificates," that protected the holders to a certain extent by ensuring them work. It is likely that Zlata's father had such a certificate. For more, see Tory, A., p. 48; USHMM, p. 243; Mishell, W.W., pp. 59 & 77; and Baran, R. (2017).

8. Tory, A., pp. 67 & 88.

9. Tory, A., pp. 114-115 & 132; USHMM, p. 245. According to Steve Aronson, the doctor who came to the house to deal with Eta's pregnancy was possibly Dr. Vidovski.

10. Mishell, W.W., p. 139.

11. See Elkes, J., p. 39; Littman, S., pp. 96-112; and USHMM, p. 244.

12. See Faitelson, A.; Gempel, B.; Littman, S., pp. 111 & 180; Mishell, W.W., p. 199; Oshry, E., p. 115; and USHMM, p. 208.
13. See Gabis, R., p. 351; Mishell, W.W., p. 204; and USHMM, p. 244; Gar, pp. 203-215.
14. Aunt Reva remembers that most of the ghetto prisoners would assemble in *brigadas* (work groups) early in the morning at the front gate, to be taken out to work. When the announcement came that the ghetto was closed, she was quickly sent to the house of the Santocki's to be hidden with Eta, Nechama and Genya in a prepared *malina* (bunker) under the house.

FORBIDDEN WEDDING IN THE GHETTO

It was already 1944, just before the end of the ghetto. How unusual that under these circumstances, we decided to get married. Why would we bother to get married when it was a time when lives were being ended? Well, we were thinking, if we survive ... okay, we will be together. If we won't survive, so we were together for a short time. Only three couples we knew had married officially by a Rabbi in the ghetto, the rest just joined together as a couple—and they were married—period! My mother thought I was crazy for wanting to get married at such a time, but my father was happy about it. My father believed that we should get married officially. I had over-heard my father telling my mother that he would like to see me get married the right way. That's why I did it.

So what did my parents arrange for us? My father brought Rabbi Oshry, and my mother made some food; it was a Sunday, June 4, 1944. My three sisters and Reva, my new sister-in-law, held up a tablecloth as a *chuppa* [wedding canopy]. Aside from our parents and sisters, we invited the people closest to us: my mother's cousins from the little house, an uncle and an aunt of the Sidrers, and a couple who were our friends, Itke Einich and his first wife.[1]

We also had to invite the mother and sister of Sia, who lived with us. Just to let you know what a terrible woman she was, in the middle of our wedding she declared that: "My son was supposed to be in his [Liova's] place ... under the *chuppa*." Can you imagine that?

In those years a wedding was different than now. Today, the parents take the couple to the *chuppa* [wedding canopy], but then it was the *unterfirer* [best wo/man] who took the couple to the *chuppa*. The *unterfirer* had to be close family members and had to be in their first marriage. So we had an uncle and the aunt from the Sidrer side, and from my side, I had the Einichs. We had a *chuppa* ceremony and *zehuzeh* [Hebrew: that was it]—we were married. And that was the end of it.

I will tell you of an interesting coincidence. Rabbi Oshry survived the war. When the South African Jewish community heard that a Lithuanian Rabbi had survived the Holocaust, they sent him a ticket and invited him to come to Johannesburg, because most of the Jews of South Africa are of Lithuanian heritage. One day he was telling the community his stories from the Kovno ghetto. He was describing the hardships, but despite it all there was happiness— and he proceeded to tell the story of a wedding over which he presided. He mentioned the name: Sidrer. One of the community members fainted when he recognized the name—it was my mother-in-law's, Chaya's, brother [Kamionski], who had immigrated to South Africa before the war.

After the wedding, my husband came to live with us in my parents' tiny apartment. If the tiny apartment wasn't small enough with the three girls, my mother and father—now there was me and my new husband. So we made a little corner for ourselves behind a curtain. We continued working in the *werkstaten*—but, we were clever too; we switched to the night shift which left us alone in the house together during the day time.

We got married on June 4, 1944, but we had a short married life together. On June 13, we had to say goodbye to each other as Liova came to tell me that he had a possible opportunity to escape from the ghetto. That was almost at the end, just before the liquidation of the ghetto.

---

1. Baran, R. (2017): "... the wedding took place in the Santocki home because they had a larger front room. Liova's friends guarded all the streets around the Santocki house ... and used a secret whistle to warn of danger."

LIOVA'S ESCAPE AND LIBERATION

One day, the Germans closed the ghetto completely; no one could go out or come in and nobody could go to work. [1]This was the first week of July 1944 [July 8, 1944].[2] We walked around the streets with some friends, wondering what would happen next and where we would wind up. We knew that something was going to happen. No one could go out or come in. We gathered in the *werkstaten*.

During those days, a group of Germans stopped by the *werkstaten* and asked for mechanics to help fix their trucks, which were in a garage outside the ghetto. It was evidently very urgent as they were preparing to leave soon. The battlefront was approaching from the east; the Russians were coming closer to the city and the Germans panicked. They came to ask for volunteers and Liova and three other men said they were the best mechanics.

Before boarding the trucks to take them out of the ghetto, Liova just managed to find me and tell me about this opportunity to escape. I told Liova that since he was a mechanic he should go. I told him: "If you are smart, you won't come back." He never forgot what I told him ... and he never came back—until after the liquidation of the ghetto. That was the seventh of the seventh—[it was] July when he ran away. I met the wife of the other friend; we didn't know what to do. Another woman did not let her husband go.

After our reunification, the following year, Liova told me what had happened during and after his escape. I didn't know anything about this until much later.

They were taken to a garage in another town [Raudondvaris] and began fixing the trucks. They were being guarded by two Germans. Between themselves they quietly strategized their escape. At the first opportunity, they decided that they would each make a run for it. As soon as one guard left the area, they ran and jumped over a big fence and continued running towards a main road, through fields leading to the forest. They divided up and ran in different directions; two of them reached the woods. Upon revisiting this fence after the war, Liova showed me the fence; he could never understand how he managed to climb over it.

Liova never planned on going to the woods because he wanted to go back to Kovno to *goyim* [non-Jews] who he knew would help him out. So, he hid in the corn [tall wheat] fields and was able to overhear how the Germans were searching and asking farmers if they saw some runaway Jews. Luckily, there were no scout dogs and no one noticed Liova running or hiding. After nightfall, he got up, removed the yellow star from his jacket and walked toward the main road. Nobody stopped him; nobody was around and he walked right into Slabodka, which is where the ghetto was.

He went straight to the house of a woman who had worked for his father in the old factory.[3] She lived in a building nearby. When she saw him, she hid him in the [Sidrer] factory attic. She fed him every day and he stayed there. She brought him food and told him to remain there until further notice. Luckily, he found books in the attic which he could read.

He remembered the words of an *izvotchik* [a horse and carriage driver]—a *Kovner goy* [non-Jew from Kovno] who promised to help him if he ever got into trouble. Liova found his house and knocked at his door; upon seeing him, the *izvotchik* took him into the attic, gave him food, and told him to sit quietly. Liova stayed there a few days, until one day the *izvotchik* came running and told him that he must leave—somebody suspected that escapees were hiding out in town. He was afraid that he would be found and both their lives would be in jeopardy.

Liova left and decided to try and cross the bridge into Kovno. The *izvotchik*'s house was not far from the bridge and across the bridge, right on the other side, was the Sidrer family's first factory, located on the Kovno side of the river. Liova knew this place very well and knew people who might help him.

He waited and observed the German guards on the bridge for a while and when he felt the time was right, he walked nonchalantly across the bridge, saying hello to the guard, and walked right into Kovno—in broad daylight.

During his week in this new hiding place near the bridge, he had a view of the surroundings through cracks in the walls. He could see the streets; he could hear the fighting between the Germans and Russians. He saw the Russians approaching the city and observed a big battle. He watched the Germans run away and saw the first Russian soldiers cross the Slabodka bridge. He observed the whole thing.

When the Russians approached, he jumped out of his hiding place to greet the first Russian soldier who entered on a motorcycle; he wanted to thank him for saving his life. In retrospect, this spontaneous action could have been his end, as they could have killed him at that moment. That was how he was liberated on August 1, 1944. He eventually found himself a job in the city archives and continued his life under Russian occupation, waiting for the rest of Europe to be liberated by the Allies.

---

1. Sidrer, Liova told the author about his escape from the ghetto in 1987. Parts of his story can be found in Chapter II, interspersed in the section on Lithuania.

2. USHMM, p. 248.
3. Sidrer, R., described this woman who was a laborer during the construction of Feival's factory. She was a stone-carrier. Feival found her crying one day because she didn't have enough money to pay the tuition for her son's schooling. Feival gave her money to pay the tuition until the end of the year. She fed and hid Liova when she found him in the attic, along with her son who was also in hiding.

LIQUIDATION OF THE KOVNO GHETTO

In early July 1944 [July 13] they started moving everyone out of the ghetto to concentration camps at either Stutthof [for women] and Dachau [for men].[1] Some were sent to other camps, such as Bergen-Belsen or Auschwitz. At that time there were only 8,000 Jews remaining in Kovno. Imagine that—8,000 out of 35,000![2] They began taking us to trains. Everyone knew what the trains meant so many tried to hide in *malinas.*

The whole area of the ghetto was the oldest section of Kovno. It was made up of single or attached houses of two or three rooms each. However, there was a block of three-story buildings, under which they built *malinas.* The hiding rooms were well prepared, with everything, and when the Germans did break into the house, the Jews were safely hidden downstairs. In some cases, people didn't even know they were free until someone came to tell them to come out. Some had very good hiding places and they survived; whole families survived like Liova's friend Leibowitz with his family. These were the only *malinas* in the ghetto with survivors because they were under these big buildings with three stories. All the other *malinas* were destroyed in the subsequent fires; all the other residents died in the fires.

Our friends, the Ipsons, also survived in their *malina* outside the ghetto, hiding underground under a potato field. They invited other members of their family to hide and survive with them.[3]

My sister Ida had quite a few boyfriends in the ghetto; one was much older than her. He was in love with her and begged her to hide in his family's *malina*, however, she didn't go with him. Ironically, he took someone else to his *malina* and survived with his family. In our backyard there was another house where our cousin and family lived. They took someone else into the *malina* and they also survived. Our cousins Chadash set to preparing themselves a *malina* and my sister, Ida, joined them with her new boyfriend, Tiktin, who she really fell in love with. Unfortunately, the Germans blew up and burned down many of the houses and this one was also destroyed.[4] Four people were killed in that basement and this is how I lost Ida. She was born on September 2, 1927 and died in July 1944.

Liova had successfully escaped two days before the liquidation of the ghetto. After his liberation by the Russians [August 1, 1944], he returned to the burned-out ghetto site. He met some of the luckier survivors as they came out of their *malinas*. Some were friends. All joined together to help bury the dead. In reconnoitering around the site, he came to the little house where we lived; it was also partially destroyed. In it he found a part of the dress I was wearing when we said goodbye. He thought that I was dead even though he did not find a corpse, but in actual fact, I had changed clothes at the last minute before we left the ghetto. Little did he know that I would come back.

When the liquidation of the ghetto and relocation began, 1944 in July, I was staying with the Sidrers and not with my parents. Why did I stay with the Sidrers and not my family? The Sidrers were offered a hiding place in the ghetto. They accepted and I went into hiding with them. I remained in the *malina* one night during which time we almost died, all of us, because there was no air; we couldn't breathe. I was terribly upset; I told Feival: "We are going to die here.

We must get out." We all climbed out and were caught. They took us to that place where they typically collected the Jews in the ghetto; we sat under some trees and we remained there overnight. The following morning, we were among the first ones to be taken to the trains.

---

1. Elkes, J., p. 108.
2. Sources indicate that there may have been as few as 6,100 left. See USHMM, p. 211.
3. A model of the ghetto and the hiding place under the potato field can be visited at the Virginia Holocaust Museum, established and directed by Jay Ipson, the child survivor from this story.
4. Yad Vashem research states that "According to different sources between 1,000 to 2,000 Jews were shot during the liquidation of the Kaunas ghetto on July 7-12, 1944. The ghetto was burned and hiding places were destroyed by explosives. On July 13, 1944 about 300-400 Jewish ghetto inmates were discovered in hiding and shot, along with some elderly and ill Jews. The perpetrators were Kaunas city Gebietskommissar Cramer; commander of Einsatz Kommando 3, Jäger; commander of the Kaunas ghetto, Jordan; Gestapo commander in Kaunas, Rauca; Einsatzkommando 3; commander of Kaunas city and region, Bobelis; the mayor of Kaunas, Palciauskas; members of the 1st Lithuanian Police Battalion led by Šimkus; and members of the Lithuanian Activist Front."

DEPORTATION TO THE CONCENTRATION CAMPS

Needless to say that when we saw the trains, we knew what this meant. We were put into a train; it was standing room only. We were holding on to each other so that we would not fall; and the train began moving. We travelled the whole day and the whole night. People were screaming and crying; there was no food and nothing to drink. I fell asleep on some man's shoulder; I don't even know who he was. When I woke up I didn't know where I was. I was next to Feival, Chaya and Reva and around noontime the train stopped. All the women were taken off the train at a concentration camp [July 13, 1944], but the men remained on the train and continued to another place. We did not know it at that time, but the men were going to another camp. Both my father and my father-in-law would meet up in Dachau.

SURVIVAL IN STUTTHOF
CONCENTRATION CAMP

The train left and we were hoarded into camp. This camp is located near Danzig [Gdansk], in the Polish corridor between Poland and Germany. Stutthof was an old camp which originally housed criminals. It was originally a prison but they also had a crematorium. When we arrived we saw the crematorium which was active at one time; it was not active while we were there. After disembarking from the trains, we sat on the ground. The summer heat was terrible.

They took groups of women into a barrack full of doctors and everyone had to be examined. Everyone had to undress. Everything was taken away from us. Adult women were examined even in their vaginas, in case they were hiding something there. I did succeed in hiding the only thing I had of value—my wedding band. I refused to give it up and began a hiding game. When they examined me internally, I held it in my hand; when they examined my mouth, I hid it in my hair, so I saved my wedding ring. During the whole time that I was in the camps, I kept a *shmate* [rag] wrapped around my finger to cover my precious wedding ring. People asked why and I said I had a cut.

After they checked me, it was Reva's turn. She began to scream.

Chaya, my mother-in-law, pleaded with the guards to leave her alone; she was only 12 [she was 15]. They relented and did not examine her. After the examinations, we went into another room and they gave us other clothes [striped uniform]. We were then sent to the barracks and we stayed there until everyone was checked.

One day later they asked for volunteers to register the incoming prisoners—*shreibers* [registrars]. My mother-in-law said: *"Zlatke gey"* [Zlata, you go]. So I went. We were about ten women. They brought us into a big room—a barrack—and gave us ledgers. First we had to register our own names and we received a number; mine was #41410. We were among the first ones from our group. Later people received higher numbers. After a full day, we completed all the names of our entry group and were supposed to return to our barracks. Then, a new transport arrived and we had to return to register them immediately.

All of a sudden, I saw my mother and my two sisters arrive. Imagine! I, myself, registered them into the concentration camp![1] The Germans started making their "selections." They sent Nechama to one side by herself, and my little sister, Genya, who was 11 at that time, to a different place. My mother would not allow Genya to be separated from her, so she joined her on the "other" line. I immediately sent Nechama to be with the Sidrers so she would not be alone. I was not sure what was going to happen to my mother and little sister. At that time, we didn't know what was happening really.

I remember that my mother was cold, so I went over to one woman and asked if she had an extra sweater. I gave it to my mother. They took them away and I never saw them again. We frantically began to inquire as to their whereabouts. We were told that they were taken to another camp—that's all. After the war, we learned that they were taken to Auschwitz.[2] I had feared that, but was not sure until 2004 when I learned for sure. Every time I see a documentary showing children at Auschwitz, I always look at each child to see if I could recognize Genya. I always believed that if my mother were with me in camp she would have survived; if I survived, she would have survived. Rivka and Chaya were together and they survived. But it wasn't meant to be. That thought never leaves me. Had she been with me she would have survived—but she wouldn't give up her child.

At the next roll call, while standing according to our numbers, we were divided again and some were sent to different work camps. I then realized why they separated the children from the adults— this was a work camp. I was separated from Chaya, Reva and Nechama and I was sent to work in one of these working camps. As we were lined up according to our numbers, I was placed next to a girl from Kovno, Henny Aronson [#42018]. My greatest fear was to be all alone. From that moment on, she and I stuck together. "You're alone, I'm alone," so we stayed together throughout the whole *shpiel* [play/event] with a few other women. We worked to stay alive and we kept each other alive. That was in August 1944 and we worked together until this camp closed on January 15, 1945.

We were fed—whatever they fed us, how much did they feed us? Well, in the morning, we got some brown water which was supposed to be coffee. Actually, my fear of getting lice was so great that the dirty brown water we were given to drink in the morning I used instead to wash my hair. I believed that lice caused disease and that I had to keep myself clean. We helped each other keep clean. For example, one day I got my hair washed with my "coffee" and the next day I washed Henny's hair with hers.

In the evenings we got a bowl of watery soup. Once a day we were given bread plus a *"teenchy"* little piece of margarine; that's why I never touch margarine to this day. They used to give out loaves of bread to different groups of women. My girlfriends often chose me to cut the bread because I was a "good cutter." We had to cut it up among us and God-forbid somebody should get a piece which was a millimeter bigger than another's. Once the women almost killed me because when I cut the loaf, one slice was off by a little. That was our diet and that was our life.

We used to go to work in the morning. I always believed that work would keep me alive—and work I did. We were sent to dig ditches —not just a ditch—but tremendous big ones against tanks, so when a tank crossed it would fall inside and it can't get out anymore. In each place, that's what we did. We were transported by train and by trucks to work in various places, perhaps to five or six camps. Sometimes we slept outdoors in tents, sometimes inside in barracks.

We worked and worked and dug and dug those anti-tank trenches. We were divided into work groups. There were three station levels. The one on the bottom would shovel and send the soil up to the station above and the one from the second station would send it up to the top. Since I was the younger one in the group I was sent down deeper into the pit and brought up the soil; I was always on the bottom, which was lucky for me because nobody watched over me and it was warmer down there.

We were working way out in the fields. There was no place to run, hide or escape. It was a completely open field with no villages anywhere in sight. Sometimes we would see groups of Greek prisoners walk by. Sometimes they threw us a cigarette. I remember the black uniforms of the SS guards who watched us. I used to know all their names but can't remember now. We became adept at stealing. When we worked digging those tank trenches we would sneak off and dig up turnips. Once I got caught coming out of the field with the vegetables and got beaten for it. I continued working, so I guess the beating wasn't so bad.

On the way we stayed in tents—not little tents but big round tents with about 50 women per tent. There was a heater in the middle and that helped a little; it was always below freezing outside. We used to stand around the heater and warm ourselves.

We were a group of five: Yocheved was older—she was a nurse; and there were Henny, her sister-in-law and another nurse and myself. The five of us stayed together. We slept together on the ground which was covered with straw; all five of us stayed warmer together and piled our five measly blankets on top of our bodies. If one of us had to turn, all of us had to turn. We tried to keep each other's spirits up by laughing at our situation, but it was bad. Henny and I used to dream and talk about life after the war. Our vision of heaven was: a loaf of bread to cut or tear as we wanted, American cigarettes to smoke, and Russian music to listen to.

I remember one young girl who was together with her mother in the barracks. The mother was crying all the time. It bothered me so because I was jealous that this girl had her mother with her. As I said, I always believed that if my mother were with me, she would have survived ... but she chose to stay with the baby, Genya, and they were sent to their deaths in Auschwitz.

Interestingly, there was not too much sickness. Our diet was very poor so I really don't know what the reasons—but we stayed healthy. We were determined to stay clean and free of lice because we believed that lice will kill you. But when do you get lice? When you are strong and healthy your body fights the lice. You get lice when your resources are depleted ... and ours were certainly so. Oh God, when I think of it. But some of us started getting the dreaded lice. One day, on our way to work, Henny and I saw a puddle of frozen water. We guarded each other so as not to be seen and we broke the ice, undressed and washed ourselves. I was so skinny, I lost a lot of weight, but I was strong and I kept working all the time.

At first, the weather was still warm so the work wasn't "so" bad. However, by November, it started to get colder and winter came, and European winters are just awful. That's when the trouble started. I had no shoes and I had no coat; none of us had. So we started screaming bloody murder. For most of the time I wrapped newspapers around my feet but we still had to go and dig. It was so difficult and painful; and they watched us every minute. We worked every single day like that in those inhumane conditions.

One day the Germans received a truckload of old clothes. I was the lucky one to get a coat. I wanted to make a bra, so I tore out part of the lining of the coat. So, how do you make a bra without needle and thread? Somebody, I don't remember who, had a needle. So we would pass it around. Scissors nobody had. So we used to tear instead of cut. I made a bra to keep myself warmer. You would have been proud of me.

I remember that at one time I had a terrible *farunkle* [abscess] on my elbow; I thought I would go out of my mind with pain. I was standing at *Appel* [roll call] and I don't know what happened, maybe I wasn't standing right and suddenly an officer named Max walked over to me and gave me such a *knack* [hard blow] and opened up the *farunkle* on my elbow. I fainted. I found myself in the barrack, with my mother-in-law taking care of me. Once the *farunkle* was opened, the pain stopped. Luckily, this happened before we were sent to work.

---

1. State Museum, Stutthof, Certificate, May 25, 1999. The prisoner numbers are recorded as: Eta 43527; Nechama 43529; and Genia 43528. All were transported on the same day—July 13, 1944. This information was requested by Zlata Sidrer in 1999 and confirmed by the author in 2017.
2. My research has revealed that they actually arrived by train directly to the gas chambers and crematorium and were murdered immediately at Birkenau, the camp a few kilometers from Auschwitz. Their ashes were most likely strewn in the pond nearby.

THE DEATH MARCH

We worked like this till January 1945, all the while trying to stay alive.[1] In January we realized that the Russians were approaching. Suddenly, the Germans packed us up and took us out. From January until March 10 we were marched through the countryside during the awful Polish winter. This was known as the death march.

Typically, the Germans had a practice of moving the Jews whenever the enemy was approaching. This happened from the ghetto and also from the concentration camps during the death march. Whenever the Russians started approaching, they moved their prisoners in a different direction away from the advancing forces. Their aim was for more prisoners to die during the relocation. Had they fled and left us alone, we all would have survived. Ironically, those who remained at Stutthof were liberated earlier by the Russians and were never taken on a march, so they all survived.[2]

We lost so many people on this march. They were very weak and exhausted. Many collapsed and then they froze to death; their eyes were still open but they were dead. One minute they were looking at you and the next, they were gone. The Germans would shoot them right away and leave them on the road.

And we started marching in the freezing weather of northern Europe in winter. You can imagine how cold it was. We walked across a river which was entirely frozen. Even tanks crossed on the ice of the Visla [Vistula] River. I am forgetting the names of the places where we stopped every night. We walked the whole day. At night we stopped and often slept in a barn. In the mornings we would begin the march again.

When we stopped, they used to prepare some food. They knew in advance where we would be at a particular time, so they could begin cooking in advance. What was our food? They prepared soup which was water, and if you found a piece of potato in it you were lucky. It was basically hot water—that was it. We only ate once a day. I was skinny and lost a lot of weight, but I was strong. I kept working all the time and walking all the time.

We were finally given food every day. I distinctly remember that on February 5, 1945, on my birthday, we were put in military barracks of the SS and the *Wehrmacht* took over. We were sitting on the floor and I told my friends: "Hey, you know today is my birthday. I am 20 years old, and look at where I am." That was in Praust. I remember that very clearly. We warmed up a bit that night and the next morning we continued marching. The entire period of time during the march was a blur of walking and camping in different places each night. As we continued the march, we met other groups of people from different camps. After passing Praust, Poland, the SS guards in the black uniforms left us in the hands of the military who wore green uniforms.

One night, as we were sleeping in a barn, someone came to wake us up. They needed one of my girlfriends, Rochele, who was a nurse, to come with them and help out. One of the women was giving birth. No one knew she was pregnant when she arrived at the camp. She understandably kept it a secret, and now she was giving birth. I went with Rochele to help her. I held a flashlight up so she could help with the birth. I have no idea how she had a flashlight. The mother did not make a sound throughout the birth. She gave birth to a boy on this death march. Can you imagine that one? I never even knew their last names. We just wrapped the baby in the only clean blanket we had, which was full of lice.

The next morning, we had to continue marching again. But you gotta keep a baby quiet. The first house she saw, she ran out and gave the baby away. She knew that neither she nor the baby would survive this situation. She remembered where and what and how and said that if she survived she would come back for the baby. After liberation, she did go back but she never found her baby.

We continued until we arrived at a prison. They let us camp there for the night. We went wild there. It was so warm and beautiful, but you see, when the body is cold in freezing temperatures, the lice are not that active, but when it is warm, the lice start working on you. We had body lice, not just head lice, and that's what brings disease —and it did.

I was the happiest one when we arrived at this prison because I found a pair of men's rubber boots. No one could imagine my happiness. I walked as if I was walking to a dance. That was unbelievable, and that's how we walked until we came to Chinov [Chynowie].

On the march to Chinov, we suffered a great disappointment. Rochele ran away and left us; she just disappeared. We found out, years later, that she decided that she had had enough and she ran to a house; they took her in and she survived. We were angry at her. We felt that we were going through this together and were very upset to learn that she just picked herself up and ran away without saying a word. We had to look for her; we were worried.

We camped in a tremendous, tremendous barn. It must have been March 1 or 2, because on March 10 we were liberated. We must have camped in this one spot for approximately eight to nine days. That was when everybody got sick. Each morning they would pull out dead bodies and dump them in a huge hole in the back, in a field behind the barn. We were still being guarded by the same Germans in the green uniforms, not black. We had food every day, but the majority of our women died of typhus at that time. That was when Henny's friend's mother died—right in that barn. We did not allow the Germans to *shlep* out her body; we took one of our blankets and we carried her out ourselves and put her into the hole.

Then Henny got sick. While she was sick I nursed her. I kept a little bottle of water between my legs to keep it warm. I would continuously put drops of water on her lips, as she had a very high fever. The fever was so high you didn't know what you were saying. Typhus is a terribly contagious disease, but she overcame it. I was the next one to get sick and she took care of me. And this is how we stayed there for maybe ten days, I don't know.[3]

---

1. For more information about the events in this chapter, see Drywa, D., which includes the map of the towns on the "Evacuation Routes": Mikoszewo, Klein Zunder, Praust, Niestepowo, Burggraben, Przodkowo, Pomieczyno, Lebno, Luzino, Wejherowo and Chynowie.
2. This comment was wishful thinking for Zlata. They suffered so much on the death march, and lost so many women, that Zlata believed that those who remained in the camp were better off and were liberated earlier. Neither Zlata, nor my aunt, Reva, ever met anyone who had survived the last days in Stutthof. The facts were that very few of the prisoners who remained behind in the camp survived and, Zlata's column was liberated on March 10, while those in Stutthof were only liberated on May 9th, 1945. (USHMM, nd)
3. Testimonies by Blackman Slivka, R., Aronson, H. and Galperin Godin, N. corroborate Zlata's memories of the death march. Aronson described the barn in Chynowie as "Dante's Inferno."

LIBERATION AND BEYOND

One morning one of the women woke early and went outside the barn. She noticed that there were no guards. She came running back, opened the big door and started screaming: "The Germans are gone! There are no Germans around here!" Everybody ran outside and sure enough, all the Germans had left in the middle of the night. By the evening the Russians arrived.[1]

We didn't wait. We ran directly into the nearest little village. It was a small town approximately 2-3 kilometers from Chinov [Chynowie] and it had been evacuated. We entered various houses and they were empty; no one was left. We realized that they had left in a rush because the food on the table in some of the houses was still warm —everybody ran. These were Germans and Poles; they were afraid of the Russians.

Of course, the first inclination of a starving person is to gorge yourself on food when it becomes available, however, Yocheved, who was a nurse, wouldn't let us eat certain things or allow us to eat quantities. She knew that we shouldn't start eating immediately or we would die. We had to start eating slowly and only the right food because our stomachs had completely shrunk. Yocheved watched over us carefully and she saved our lives with her professional advice, because some people grabbed the first available food, like milk from cows, and they died from that.

Due to the disease in the town the Russians enforced a quarantine. No one in and no one out. There was a hospital in this town. Our friend, Yocheved, was insane with a fever from typhus, so we *shlepped* [carried] her to the local hospital. She was lucky, at least she had a hospital—Henny and I got through it [typhus] in a barn.

The Russians helped out a little bit. They gave us food. But, even so, many people died after liberation, especially those who were sick. For example, I met the daughter of some family friends, Mofshovitz. She told me that her mother had just died; the next day, the girl was dead as well.

We stayed in this town until they lifted the quarantine; it must have been around the month of April when everybody got well. We were then free to move around. We used to go to the hospital, visit our sick friends, and meet people who we did not know were alive. I used to visit Yocheved in the hospital and listen to what was happening. And people started leaving. Where did they go?

We took over one of the evacuated houses that we found and we lived there together in seeming luxury. We were Henny, her sister-in-law [Tanya], Yocheved, a friend of Chayele Krieger, a cousin, another two women and myself—all in that little one-room house. And who was the cook? *Moi!* I started cooking, soups from what-ever ingredients I found. There was a lot of food in this house. We started cooking, getting healthier and stronger. While living in this house, I had a chance to look at myself in a large mirror for the first time in years. I did not recognize myself. I was bald, had no boobs and my skin was dark, like sunburned, and I was very small.

A while thereafter, we were confronted with a new threat. We heard that the Russian soldiers were looking for girls; we found out what they were doing to the girls. Then we were in trouble, but one Russian soldier came in and told us that he was Jewish. He felt sorry for us, brought us food and we posted a big sign on the door

'Typhus'. He got into the one bed with all four of us with his rifle and wouldn't let anyone in. We always talk and laugh about this event when we get together and reminisce.

We stayed quite a while in this town, until they declared that we were free to return to our homes. A few women from our group decided to return to Kovno. One of them was the sister of my friend, Simcha Gerber. Before she left, I told her: "Just in case you get to Kovno and just in case you see my husband, please tell him I am alive." She said she would. That was my first message to my husband. At the time, I had no idea whether he survived. At a later time, I learned that he did get this message.

We stayed a few more weeks and then told the Russians that we wanted to leave too. They actually offered to take us back to Kovno, but first they wanted us to work for them a little longer and then they would take us home to *Lita* [Yiddish: Lithuania]. We decided to take advantage of this offer, as we had no other means. We were six women who wanted to go to Kovno. They took us by train to Gdinya, a port city [near Gdansk, Poland]. The Germans were still on the [offshore] island but the rest of the surroundings were under the Russians. Gdansk is a magnificent city. They took us there and gave us a beautiful large room in a beautiful building where the six women all slept in the same room. They gave us food, beds to sleep in and we worked for them. What did we have to do? Milk cows. Now picture it—Zlata and Henny milking cows. They soon realized that we were city girls and knew nothing about farm work, so they removed us from cow detail.

They then took us to a big, tremendous building which was once a school. Each floor had different kinds of things. One floor had all kinds of electrical appliances, another was full of barrels with green liquid soaps, one was full of flags, dishes, and furniture. This was all the loot from the people who were captured and killed by the Germans. They were sending it back home to Germany, but didn't manage to take it all out—it was so much. Now the Russians wanted to take it back to Russia.

However, the *Polaks* [Polish people] who lived around knew exactly what was in this building and came to steal it. The Russians realized that they had to have someone guard this treasure, and we became the guards. We guarded until one day they started shooting at us. Of course, we ran away. We told the captain: "How do you expect us to guard if we are being shot at?" So, they gave us rifles; but, of course, none of us knew how to shoot. So, they taught us how to shoot—and we learned to shoot very well. We guarded mostly at night. This time when someone started shooting, we shot back—even without taking aim. They were afraid; they didn't know who we were. This is what we did.

Now, since we all had nothing to wear, we took some of the flags from the warehouse storage and used the material to make clothes. We asked for needle and thread and Henny made a blouse. The flag fabric was scratchy and very unpleasant.

Sundays we would go for walks and sometimes the Russians took us all together to the movies. They picked us up and paid for us. One day, the four of us were walking in town and saw a young man walking in front of us. He was wearing a long shoulder bag and we realized that he was not a local man. We followed him and whispered the code word question: "*Amcho?*" [Are you a member of the tribe?] He turned around with acknowledgement. He was.

We thought we were the only ones who had survived this horror; we didn't know if anyone else survived. We almost fainted to see a Jewish man for the first time; we only saw the women who were liberated with us. And so, the questions began: "Who are you? Where are you going?" He started telling us that he had been traveling for weeks by train, walking and hitchhiking from the Lithuanian cities of Vilna and Kovno. We asked him if he saw anyone else alive. "Yes, there are many who are alive." I described my husband, Liova. He said that he thought he had seen him in Kovno. He also told us that Lodz was the place where many survivors were convening. He was on his way there to find information about his own family and friends.

I found a scrap of paper; I don't remember where I got it from, and wrote a *tstetele* [a note] with my name and my location on this little piece of paper. I asked him to please post this note wherever he'll be. The thought that maybe someone from our family survived was too much ... I was afraid to hope. We said goodbye; we were so happy to see a Jewish man.

We continued with our jobs as the Russians began to load all the looted goods from the building onto a big open platform with horses—and they used to take it to the train station way down the hill. They would unload and return for more. One of us always went along on the transport to guard them with our rifles. That particular day it was my turn to guard.

On this particular day, the horse driver stopped, pulled the brake and jumped off the carriage somewhere near the train station. I took out a cigarette, but had no light. I smoked non-stop. I asked the driver for a light, but he did not have one. I suddenly saw a man walking on the street we were coming down. I jumped off the wagon to ask him for a light. And who do you think it was? It was *Zeide* [grandfather] Feival, my father-in-law. How can I describe that moment in time? He just got off the train and started walking.

I started screaming hysterically; you could have heard me miles away. Feival took me by the hand and hushed me up saying: "Shhh ... don't scream. Come with me right away." So I calmed down but told him that I could not leave my friends behind. In addition, the driver of the horse and carriage was standing there, watching and waiting. Feival agreed to come with me to speak to the Russian captain. We returned to the place where we were working and to the apartment where I lived. I introduced him as my father, not my father-in-law. I told everyone that my mother and sisters survived. Feival petitioned the Russian captain for my release. He spoke to him in Russian, yet the captain told us to stay a while longer, as they wanted us to continue working for them.

Feival stayed in our room with my friends and he told us all his stories. The girls were crazy about this man. I don't remember whether at that time he told Henny and Yocheved about the fate of their parents, but he told me all the details about my father. Seeing Feival alive was a happy shock, but at the same time my hopes to see my own father were shattered. Feival was with him in Dachau and knew he had died. It is impossible to describe the feelings at such a time—to suddenly learn that my father had died but my little sister Nechama had survived the camps and the death march. Although she was in the same camp with my mother-in-law and Reva, she was not with her family, thus, in my eyes, she was alone. She was liberated in January 1945 and no one was sick in this camp. I don't know if she would have survived in our camp.

Feival also told me about my father and their experiences in the Dachau concentration camp. After the long train ride [out of Kovno], the women were dropped off the train at Stutthof, and the men continued on the train to Dachau. My father, Yankel, arrived after him, but they both met up in the camp. Feival worked with electricians at a Messerschmitt production plant. My father also had a job.

I asked Feival about what they did on Yom Kippur in Dachau. I remember being in the work camp on Yom Kippur. I don't know how the women knew it was Yom Kippur, but they did. On that day I had a dream. I dreamt that my father was singing *Kol Nidre*, as I remember he did during the last Yom Kippur in the ghetto. I asked Feival if my father sang *Kol Nidre* in Dachau. "Yes, he did," he told me. Thereafter, Yom Kippur was always the worst day for me.

It seems that my father was a heavy smoker and he bartered his ration of bread for cigarettes. He got very sick and died on March 23, 1945—it was one month before the U.S. liberation of Dachau in April [April 29, 1945]. It was so close to liberation, but he never made it. I am sorry that I didn't know enough about my father. His number in the camp was #87444.[2] I verified this information after the war from the German archives. Before we left Germany to immigrate to the U.S., I went to see the mass gravesite at Dachau to pay my respects to my papa. I never, ever, returned to Germany.

1. Mishell, W.W., p. 364, describes this time; Aronson, H. (1994, 2009): "The SS poured gasoline around the barn and planned on burning it down with everyone in it—they never managed to execute their evil design."
2. Dachau Concentration Camp Memorial Archives, Letter and Prisoner Certificate states that: "Jacob Santockis arrived Dachau July 15, 1944, arrived Kaufering I and III, transferred to subcamp Kaufering IV, died February 24, 1945... He came with one of the big transports following the clearance of Kovno. There are some published memoirs from former prisoners who were on this same transport of 1883 men together with him."

REUNIFICATION OF THE FAMILY

Feival described to me the events that led to the reunification of the Sidrer family and my sister, Nechama. From the moment of his liberation from Dachau in April, 1945 by the U.S. forces, Feival began searching for information about his family and friends. He was on his way back to Kovno by trains through Germany and Poland to look for his son, who he heard had survived and was in Kovno.

In Bialystok, he met a woman who knew Chaya and Reva from the Stutthof work group and death march. She told him that Chaya and Reva were alive and probably somewhere in Poland. He started going from town to town searching for them. He met a man who knew the Sidrer family and told him he had recognized Chaya, his wife, in a group of surviving women. Feival immediately started walking to the village which had been described to him. He came to a farm with cows and horses. It was there he found Chaya, their daughter Reva, and my Nechamale. The girls were riding horses and milking cows. Chaya was housekeeping for the Russians. They were on the Russian side.[1]

It was an almost unbelievable feat to reunite a family; this was the biggest miracle. Only my poor little sister Nechama was alone ...

my heart broke thinking of her at that moment. After Feival found them, they had to arrange for permission from the Russians to leave. Like many other survivors after the war, they managed to get to Lodz where many Jews were gathering. All this took place before they knew anything about my fate, or that of Liova.

To reunite and continue their lives, all the survivors started wandering and walking—simply walking from town to town. Sometimes they hitchhiked, caught trains, but most of the trains were military. While walking, travelling and talking to other survivors, they exchanged stories. Little by little people collected and shared information.

The Sidrers and my sister assembled at a gathering place in Lodz. There they met survivors who were just coming out of Kovno. There was an exodus from the Russian side and those who came out warned us that once you go back, you will never get out again. This message was spread by word of mouth, in addition to the information about who had survived and who had perished.

I found out later who survived and who didn't, but at the time, my main objective was to get back to Kovno. We all remembered the promises we made when we said goodbye to each other. We said that if we survived, we would meet back at home. But we could never imagine how the war would end with Europe being partitioned among different nations. To return to Kovno was now a big challenge. Some of us were in Germany, some in Poland and some back in Kovno. At the time of my liberation I did not know about anyone else who had survived.

It was in Lodz that Feival discovered that I was alive in Gdinya, through that *tsetele* [little note] on a notice board. He immediately got on a train and came to look for me. It was that moment when he got off the train when I asked him for a light for my cigarette. After I calmed down from the shock of the coincidence and the realization that he was alive, I learned that Feival had found the *tsetele* I gave to that Jewish man, who posted it on a noticeboard in Lodz. How lucky can one be?

Meanwhile, we had to go to work every day under the Russians, but Feival continued trying to persuade the captain, who finally gave us permission to leave. The other girls decided that they would take the first opportunity to run away and get to Lodz too. They would need a little money for a train ticket. We took whatever *shmattes* [rags] they owned and we told them we would meet in Lodz. We left on the next train to Lodz.

That was where I was reunited with my mother-in-law, Chaya, sister-in-law [Reva] and my little sister, Nechamale. She was the only person left from my family. At that time, I did not know the exact fate of the rest of the people in my family, except for my father.

Now that we had all reunited in Lodz, we had a few more problems: no money, no food and no work. At that time a few young survivors organized themselves into a *kibbutz* in Lodz. I knew the head of this group and asked them to take the two young girls [Nechama and Reva] into the kibbutz so they should at least have some food, as little as there was.

We lived together in the hall of the Jewish community of Lodz and everyone slept on the floor. Everyone went out looking for work, looking for people; no one was helping us with anything. Feival was looking for people. I went around looking for work. In the same complex in which we were sleeping someone established a newspaper printing business. This press office had a restaurant for workers and I got a job cleaning toilets and floors. Washing toilets is wonderful, as long as you get food. People in the kitchen let us take home food, for example, end pieces of the loaf of bread, and leftover raw dough to make *lokshen* [noodles]. We were happy we had food. Chaya made *kugels* [quiche] from the *lokshen*. This is how we lived for quite a while in Lodz.

In the meantime, my friends arrived after running away [from Gdinya]. I brought my girlfriends to the back door of the restaurant and gave them food. Little by little everyone went their own way.

Henny, who had also been married in the ghetto, was reunited with her husband in Lodz.

Feival ran around looking for people and information. We had no information about Liova. Suddenly, Feival met a friend who came from Kovno. This man had been arrested with my uncle Urke in Kovno and was also sent to Siberia [by the Russians] in 1940. He was released from Siberia and returned to Kovno and then came to Lodz looking for his family. Feival asked about Liovka. "Of course, I met him." For the first time we received confirmation that he was alive. He described the difficulties of exiting the Russian side, but with money, he said, it is still possible. But he added a terrible comment to his story: "But don't wait for your son, he will never leave Kovno." He should have been shot on the spot for saying such a thing. Feival came home crying terribly because of these words. At least he's alive, so the crying stopped.

It was at that moment that I made the decision to return to Kovno to find him. I said: "If he cannot come to us, I will go to him." Feival did not know what to say. "You really want to do it? You might never get out." I realized the truth in this but felt that at least in Kovno I would be together with my husband; that was my idea. I started making arrangements to leave. But it was not as simple at it seemed. Here we were in Lodz, Poland [U.S. sector]—and I had to get into the Russian sector, which had already begun controlling entrances and exits; it was the iron curtain.

---

1. Baran, R. (2017): "We were liberated somewhere between the cities of Torun and Bydgoszcz, Poland. We were taken by the Russians to recuperate in the spa-town of Ciechocinek which is where for the first time we saw our images in these huge mirrors. We didn't recognize ourselves. In a town somewhere nearby, we were put to work by the Russians moving cows to the train to be transported to Russia. Reva and Nechama had a horse and wagon to move the cows to drink in a lake. A woman walked by and asked them if they knew Frau Sidrer. Yes! Your papa is looking for you."

SEARCHING FOR LIOVA

Feival was walking around again and met a guy who said he was going to Kovno. He had arranged for a permit to go in by himself and leave with his wife. Since he was traveling alone, we agreed that I would accompany him as his wife. So, of course, I had to first learn his name and a few things about him. We planned to leave on the eve of Yom Kippur [September 17], 1945. We went to the train station and awaited our first train.

We had tickets and a permit and we got on the train. We did not travel for too long, perhaps until the next morning, when the train stopped. We were told that the train was not going any further—no explanation was given but we had to find other transportation. It was such a *balagan* [a mess/chaos]; no one knew anything. We had a little food with us which we ate carefully. Water you can always find. It was a terrible time.

My "husband"—I thought he was a man, *vays ich vos* [yeah, right]. He was waiting for me to take care of things. He was useless, so I started running around to look for someone to ask how to get to Kovno. It was a large yard with trains going to different destinations. I was told that there was no transportation except military transport. So, I continued looking for other alternatives. One told me that there were no trains except a coal train. I thought, okay, I didn't mind sitting on coal, but my "husband" did not want to go. I insisted that I would go alone, so he came along with me. This train stopped again. By that time, my face was completely black from the coal.

I ran around the station, going from one train to another, asking in which direction they were going. Finally, I begged a stationmaster to let me get on the train which was going in the right direction. I was literally on my knees begging him. He let us get on, but this train only took us to a station about one hour from Vilna. The train stopped and everyone had to get off. It was both a military and civilian train and we had to register our names like in a prison camp. All those who wanted to return to Russia had to go through this camp. Wow! We had no choice; we had to go through. We registered as husband and wife. They gave us a place to sleep in the barracks, but who wanted to sleep with this idiot? We had to go in together; we had no choice. Then I met another woman who was not happy with her husband, so we talked and decided to switch men. I was happy as long as I did not have to be near him; I just could not stand him.

This was the last stop before entering the Russian side and everyone had to go into the camp. We were all interrogated more than once. The Russians interrogated everybody, asking: "Who, why, what did you do?" etc. My turn came and I told him that I was in a concentration camp and what I did there. They asked where I met my "husband" etc. They asked if I knew Russian or German. When they heard that I was fluent in both, they asked if I wanted to work as their interpreter. So I worked there every day, which was wonderful. We stayed in that camp and every day my fictitious husband came to look for me. "Why don't you come back?" he asked.

After the interrogation, they said they would let us know when we could leave. One day they called me in and told me I was free to go. How do we get to Vilna? They gave us a certificate which would allow us to get to Vilna. We ran like crazy to the train; we got off in Vilna. When I got off the train I finally ran away from him [fictitious husband]; I did not want to see him near me again. I ran away to find a train to Kovno but I was told that only military trains were going and that I would have to wait. Wait? When I saw a military train begin to leave the station, I decided to take a chance and jumped on. I was standing right next to it. I stood in between the cars; I was so happy. The Russian soldiers on the train started talking to me. Why do you want to go to Kovno? I told them that I was going to find my husband. It was cold and the soldiers took me inside the car.

Finally, I came to Kovno and I got off the train with all the soldiers. I can see it even now! Once I got off the train I knew where I was; it was home. I got out of the train station with my little rucksack and while I was standing there I started crying. Where do I go to look for him? I calmed myself down and I started walking on the left side of the street. I saw a soldier in a Russian uniform coming towards me and I realized that this was a very good friend of Liova's, Gedalia, who was in the partisans. I was so happy to finally see a face I knew. He asked: "Zlatke, what are you doing here?" I told him that I returned to look for Liova, my husband. This friend was on his way to the train station as he had been drafted into the Russian army. He thought that Liova had just left Kovno because he had come to say goodbye to a mutual friend, named Nechama, just the day before.

I said: "Where do I go?" He said to come to a girlfriend's house, Nechama, who was in Kovno and lived on Laisvis Aleja: "Take me to her." So I headed out to Nechama's home, hoping to stay with her. I was afraid to shock her when she opened the door so I asked Gedalia to do it. She answered the door, and he told her that Zlatke is here and she is looking for Liova. She didn't know if Liova was still in Kovno. Gedalia went to look for him all over the city. He met another one of Liova's friends. Where is Liova? What's the matter? Zlatke is here? *Oy a broch!* [Yiddish: Oh, crap!]. He went to Haim Leibowitz and asked him to look for Liova. Haim Leibowitz found

Liova and said: "I have something to tell you." Liova quickly responded: "Zlatke is here? Yes." It was a big shock for everybody that I came. Had I arrived one day later I would have missed my husband. But, an hour later, he came to me.

At that time, Liova was enjoying a happy bachelor's life, playing around with the girls in Kovno. He met the girl whose family used to take me to the opera. She couldn't believe the coincidence of this relationship. He had a good time in Kovno. He had a beautiful, non-Jewish, girlfriend yet he was secretly preparing to leave after he learned that there were survivors outside Kovno and that his parents, sister and I were alive. In those days it was very dangerous for people to know that you were making plans to leave. There were "rats" and you could get arrested if the authorities found out that you were preparing to leave. Then, suddenly I appeared and destroyed his plans to escape.

Liova had already learned that I was alive from the woman I met in Chinov [Chynowie]. When I met her, she said she was going to Kovno. I had asked her to tell Liova that I was alive. She did manage to get to Kovno, met Liova, and told him about me. He also learned that his parents and sister were alive. So, here he was, all prepared to leave and search for us when I turned up ... looking pretty horrible.

What did I look like after all those years? Due to malnutrition, I was swollen, without hair. I had an infection in my leg all the way to the bone and it was swollen. My clothes were "not for a wedding." By contrast, he looked gorgeous, slim, suntanned—he looked like a million dollars. He was always a good-looking man. He took one look at me and didn't believe it was me. I realized that he had to be crazy to come back to me; well, he came back. I looked at him awkwardly and saw that he was wearing the wedding band. I thought that, if he is still wearing the wedding band, then everything will be okay. It was a weird feeling. He was a stranger to me yet I knew him so well. I didn't even know how to handle myself. Should I jump on him or be careful? We sat next to each other and couldn't even talk. I looked horrid and when you are upset, you look worse. And he was absolutely gorgeous. It took a while to warm up and get closer to each other.

I think he was happy to see me again—after all, I was alive—but he had a major problem. He had prepared a permit to leave for only one person. He had to pay a *macher* [someone who arranges papers] for the false travel documents as he was escaping illegally from the country. He had already sold all his belongings and suddenly I arrived. Had I come the next day I would not have found him. He was upset because I had screwed up his plans. The first thing he did was to sell the ticket to someone who wanted to get out. He found a friend and offered him the ticket. This guy had no money to pay, so Liova told him that he could repay him after they get out of Lithuania; he never did.

Now we were both in Kovno with no money and no place to stay. He had to go back to his girlfriend's house to get his belongings. We both stayed at my friend Nechama's with her family for a while. We left their house because it was so crowded and uncomfortable. How long can one stay in a place where there is no room?

We had no permanent place to live so we had to move from house to house, sleeping and eating in different places. One day, he said: "Let's go eat dinner." There was a Jewish family who prepared food and people came to eat there. It was Friday and there was a Friday menu. He took me there to eat real homemade food, including soup with *kneidlach* [soup balls], chicken, *tsimmes* [cooked carrots], *gefilte* [stuffed] fish, *compote* [cooked fruit soup] and a drink. He ordered two portions. I was eating and eating while he was watching me. I ate without stopping or even looking up. He stopped eating as he was amazed how I could eat like this. He said he couldn't finish his meal, so I finished everything from his plate too. Ever since that time, he always kidded me about "you and your appetite."

It's interesting how I just remembered that scene, after so many years. I remember how he sat and looked at me as if I came from another planet ... there were big differences between us. He and I had different experiences and feelings. For example, in later years when we were in the U.S. he used to go to Germany for work. I cringed. "How do you feel about going to Germany?" He felt okay, but I was upset that he did not have the same feelings about the war as I did. He didn't lose anybody in the war so he never knew the feeling of losing his family; I lost almost everyone. So there were differences. I forgave him for a lot of things ... That's the story.

Another thing happened the first evening after our reunion. He put his hand in his pants pocket and pulled out a pocket watch and chain and put it on the table for me. When I identified the watch I began to scream and cry hysterically. It was my father's watch. The last time I saw it was in the ghetto when my father gave it to Liova to fix because it wasn't working. As it turned out, Liova still had it in his pocket a few days later when he made his sudden escape from the ghetto, and here he was, returning it to me. It was an invaluable gift and the only tangible memory of my father. Unfortunately, this cherished memory was stolen from me in Landsberg by one of our guests. I never had proof against the thief and therefore could not accuse him or retrieve it.

At one point, we went back to my parents' house, *Auf dem Grinem Barg*, which was occupied by our Russian neighbors. I told them that we had no place to stay and they let us stay with them. I slept on the same bed that I slept on when it was our home. My mother was very fond of crystal, so I peeked into the buffet cabinet and saw that it was filled with crystal bowls, liquor glasses and many other things that my mother left. It was fantastic to see, but I made believe I didn't see it—even though it hurt terribly. The wife lied to me and said she didn't have the crystal, but I saw it in the buffet; I decided not to say anything as they were housing and feeding us— and I ignored these issues. After all she had done for us I decided not to ask her to return more of my mother's belongings.

Suddenly the wife brought out the Santocki family photo and gave it to me. My mother had given it to her to keep for after the war. It was very wrinkled because it was kept hidden in a mattress as she was afraid that someone might recognize it if they came to take things away from them. They knew Jews left a lot of good stuff. For me, it was the biggest treasure to receive this picture.

We stayed with them for a long time; they housed and fed us. While we stayed there, I developed a total body itch; it was some sort of skin disease. It was very contagious and my husband got it too. We had to go to a doctor who prescribed a black salve which we had to use to cover the whole body from the toes to the head. We kept *shmearing* [spreading]. It was horrid but we had to get rid of it. Meantime, my leg infection was getting worse. We went to a doctor and he gave me medication. We had no money to pay his fee. Papa [Liova] had no money because he stopped working. So I returned to the lady we were staying with, in my house, and asked her to give me the chandelier to pay the doctor. I brought the chandelier to the doctor as payment—and he took it. It took a long time to get rid of this body disease.

One day, while walking in the street in Kovno, someone stopped me and asked if I was Zlata; she told me that my uncle, Urke [Uriel Zivov], was looking for me. I ran to find him. He was staying in a friend's house [somewhere near the Chor Synagogue] and when I first saw him I recall thinking that he was dressed like a king. During the Russian occupation in 1940, he was sent to Siberia by the Russians as punishment for capitalist action against the state. Ironically, this arrest saved his life as his entire family was murdered in his absence [after the German occupation]. When he was liberated from Siberia he moved to Moscow. He returned to Kovno with a new partner and a son. While in Kovno, Liova travelled with him to Kalvarija to look for family members, but they learned that no one survived. He eventually had a second son, Grisha, and remained in Kovno.

Laisvis Aleja, Freedom Boulevard, used to be a magnificent boulevard before the war with trees and cafes, but after the war it was changed completely. I remember walking on this street and I saw my old Latin teacher walking toward me. I recognized him but turned my head so he couldn't see me. I kept walking. I also saw a high school classmate walking with her husband and baby down the boulevard. I didn't want her to see me. I felt envy because she had a family and a normal life, smiling, walking with a baby carriage. I wanted to get out of Kovno; I was angry. I didn't want to talk to any Lithuanians; I hated them. It was a horrible year while I was waiting to get out of Kovno.

Meanwhile, Liova and I started looking for a way to leave Kovno— we have family outside, father, mother and sisters. Liova went to register for two exit permits. We waited a long time—from September to December 1946.

During this waiting period, we had no place to eat and sleep, so we went around from house to house. Friends and acquaintances gave us food or a bed for a few days. To pay for two tickets was another problem as we had no money. But we found a dentist named Dr. Baron and she had money. She found out that her son survived and was living in Israel. I told her our predicament and she agreed to lend us the money and that we would find a way to pay it back to her son in Israel. This was the money we needed to buy the tickets and leave. In later years Feival did pay it back to the son.

We continued to wait, however. Liova could not stay in the city of Kovno because he had left his job and was not allowed to be in the city without being registered. It was dangerous; we had to be careful and we couldn't trust anyone. Since the papers were supposed to be made in Vilna we had to go and return a few times, because we were supposed to leave from Vilna. We kept moving around from house to house because we were afraid of the Russian police. They arrested people for the smallest suspicion. Liova would have been a suspicious person, as he had left a good job, and was now hanging around. So we kept moving around among friends and we slept on friends' floors. I stayed with my friends, and Liova stayed with his.

ESCAPE FROM LITHUANIA

In Kovno, there was a Jewish *macher* [someone who arranges things] who made money by selling false papers. Liova paid him for two tickets and he kept going back to him for the travel documents. The *macher* kept putting us off by saying: "Only another two days, or another day, no transport today, etc." One day Liova went to the *macher* and saw his friend Berel Gempel sitting there. "What are you doing here?" "Same thing as you." He told him that there was a transport the following night and they were getting on it. However, the *macher* had just told Liova that the transport would only arrive in a few more days. Liova went back to the *macher* but this time he came with a knife, which he had made in the ghetto, and demanded to know how come we were not on tonight's train. He took out his knife and the *macher* panicked and got us the papers for the next train.

We had to get out via Vilna, so we got on a bus from Kovno. We later got on the train in Vilna with Berel and Rochele Gempel, but we had to hide in the back because there were some Russians looking for escapees. We did not look like escapees because we had no packages; we only had an empty rucksack and the Russians did not check carefully. We were afraid all the time because others were caught and sentenced to prison.

The train started moving out of the station; we were on our way, but when we got to Grodno the train stopped. This was now the new border with Poland. We had to get out and cross the border on foot. It was December 11 and it was freezing; we did not have warm clothes. At the border, they called us by our fictitious names and we answered accordingly. We had to get to another station. We walked to a farm and asked them to let us sleep overnight. I had a few junky things in my bag but Berel had vodka. We searched for a place to sleep. Berel gave vodka to a farmer and he let us sleep near the oven. Don't ask how wonderful that was. They fed us and showed us how to get to the train. It was so cold and I didn't have warm clothes.

We had to go via Bialystok, then to Warsaw, and on to Lodz to find our family. However, when we finally got to the Sidrer apartment in Lodz we learned that our family had already left. Instead of Feival and Chaya and the girls, we found Feival's youngest brother, Eli, and his wife living in the apartment instead. Uncle Eli invited all of us to stay in this apartment. We had nothing—no money, but Berel had. He had money because he had started a business in Kovno before leaving. We headed out of Lodz after a few days, en route to Munich. Berel helped us all the way to Munich.

We were traveling with false papers of Greek Jews who were returning to Greece. Once again, we had to cross borders and walk through woods. This was quite a difficult trip from Lodz but we were led and helped by the *Bricha* [the Israeli organization that helped survivors get to Palestine]. We followed them wherever they took us. We walked, then they took us by bus, then walked again. I don't remember how many borders we had to cross but we eventually arrived in Prague by train on Christmas Eve. They took us to an American military complex where American soldiers were getting ready for the holiday. We had to be careful not to speak Yiddish because we were supposed to be

Greeks. So we simply stopped speaking in order to avoid problems.

We were given gifts and food by the Americans. We stayed that night. It was warm; we had music and food and we stayed all through the holidays. They let us go for a walk around. There was lots of snow and it was beautiful. We watched youngsters carrying skis. We were so envious. We stayed there a few days and it was lovely.

Finally, after the holidays, the American soldiers took us to the train station to continue our trip to Munich. While sitting at the station, on the floor and on benches, and waiting for the train, I made a mistake and said something to Liova in Yiddish and he answered me. Some drunk overheard us and thought we were speaking German. The man kicked Liova and called him a Nazi. This was all my fault so I would not let Liova hit him back. I will never forget that. We waited a whole day for the train. We were very afraid we would be caught.

Eventually, the train came and we continued our trip. The trains were very slow and this train only went as far as a town before Munich. We were then taken in trucks and finally dropped us off at a building in Munich; we were now on our own. We said goodbye to Berel and Rochele. They remained in Munich, but we were later reunited in the DP camp. There were many Jews all around Munich and we got information from them. We met the Ipsons in Munich. We were so happy to meet such good friends. They told us that Feival and Chaya and the girls were in Landsberg am Lech which was a DP camp outside Munich. We immediately took a train in the direction of Landsberg.

It was late at night and the train stopped in a town named Sankt Ottilian, approximately 16 kilometers from Landsberg. It turned out that on this particular night the town was full of survivors from the Landsberg DP camp who were attending a concert. We found lodging in a place which looked like a hospital. We waited until the end of the concert and watched the people leaving the concert area.

Suddenly we saw our sister Reva leaving the hall. What a reunion this was! Reva's friend went back to Landsberg by bus and told the Sidrers that Reva was staying overnight because she met her brother and his wife. From all the excitement we didn't think that we could join the group and go by bus to Landsberg with them. How silly we were.

So we stayed overnight and the next morning our friend Beba Viduchinski came with a jeep to pick us up. This reunion took place on New Year's Day 1947. How can one write about such feelings? It was such a wonderful surprise for our parents. They didn't sleep the whole night in anticipation. The family had stopped hoping to see us again.

Feival and Chaya lived in a little room. They had heard that we had arrived in the neighboring town and they sent Beba to pick us up and bring us to them. They were ecstatic. Chaya washed the curtains through the night and ironed them. This has since become a Sidrer family tradition that when guests come to visit you take down the curtains and wash them. They did not expect us as they had almost given up hope that we could ever get out of Kovno. They had heard a rumor that another group of Jews were caught trying to escape from Kovno with false papers and were put in prison. They did not think we would get out of there—but we surprised them.

DP CAMP, LANDSBERG AM LECH, GERMANY

So we started our new life in Landsberg. Thousands of people from all over Europe started to come to the Landsberg Displaced Persons camp, which was sponsored by HIAS [Hebrew Immigrant Aid Society] and UNRRA [United Nationals Relief and Rehabilitation Administration]. They fed us and gave us clothing and we worked and tried to normalize our lives. I was reunited with my only surviving relative—my sister, Nechama. She floated around from family to family for a while and then joined a kibbutz and continued with her education along with her friends Reva and Chaviva. The Jews from Palestine used to knock on the doors of the houses to convince people to go to Israel/Palestine.

At first, we lived with the Sidrers in their one-room place and slept on army cots. We had one cot and Feival and Chaya shared another. Our first order of priority was to find work; we had to do something. Some people started all sorts of businesses, for example, selling cigarettes from one town to the other. We were never businesspeople, so Liova got a job as manager of the motor pool. All the American cars that belonged to the DP camp were under him, therefore, we always had transportation.

After all my dreams of becoming a doctor, I eventually got myself a job in the hospital in the camp. I was the secretary to the American manager of the hospital. I did not speak a word of English and I learned to type with one finger. This big American in uniform became Nechama's boyfriend. I loved all the doctors; I knew everyone and they knew me. I knew what was happening. I continued working for him until they closed the hospital. I remember that he wrote me an excellent letter of recommendation before we left for the U.S., indicating that I was the best secretary. I worked there for 3.5 years. I still have that letter of recommendation; it's something to see.

We finally moved out of the Sidrers' tiny apartment and got a one-room place with a little kitchen for ourselves. We had no furniture. We found a wooden crate, put a tablecloth on it and added a flower —and it was home. We had an open kitchen. In this camp we were given food, bread and cigarettes—most of us smoked in those days. We used to barter these items instead of using money—we didn't have any. As long as we were fed and dressed we were happy. We found used clothes and if they did not fit, Chaya fixed them. Most of the clothes were donations from the U.S.

During these years in the DP camp, we filled our social lives with fun activities. On Sundays we used to travel and do sightseeing. We always had transportation at our disposal because of Liova's job at the motor pool. We would socialize with our friends. Some found their spouses and others found new mates. During that time, we also learned to ski in Bechtesgarten. We always found places to go. We would go to the mountains in summer and winter. For a loaf of bread, you could sleep a night in a German's home. We went to Munich for concerts and Augsberg had a fabulous outdoor opera. It was the first time we saw Aida on an outside stage. I'll never forget that one. It was here [DP camp] for the first time that we heard a concert with Leonard Bernstein conducting. I will never forget it. We started to have fun and often we would invite Reva and Nechama to join us. Sometimes they came with their own boyfriends. We were all young and carefree. That was the first time we met Jews from other countries, like Poland and Greece. That's how we lived during those years—travel here, travel there.

Ever since Liova was a young man, he loved to build things. He was introduced to shortwave radio in his teens and since then he loved electronics and amateur radio. With this interest, one of the first things he did when we got settled in Landsberg was to get in touch with the German amateur radio club. He continued to study and learn more about amateur radio. He would always build the equipment for his radio shack and was able to communicate with the whole world. He became good friends with a lot of people over the air. Once he even had a connection with the king of Jordan who was also a radio operator. I was just getting used to this hobby at that time.

SEARCH FOR A NEW HOME AND A SIGN
OF NEW LIFE

Everyone in the camp was making their future plans. We knew we did not wish to return to Kovno, therefore, we started writing to all our relatives around the world: in North and South America, South Africa, and Rhodesia. I had an aunt in South Africa and uncle in the U.S. and another in Uruguay. I wrote to the Jewish Agency to find the addresses of my relatives and I wrote to all of them. I wanted to let them know what had happened to us and that we wanted to get out of Europe. It took a long time until we got responses. At that time, Chaya had two brothers in South Africa and two siblings in Uruguay. We were trying to get affidavits to enter any one of these countries; it really didn't matter to us where. The U.S. did not allow anyone to immigrate; they had closed the doors. South Africa had the lowest quota for Lithuanians. Many of these countries gave very few people entrance, consequently, we had to wait the longest among our friends.

One day, while I was visiting my in-laws, I was standing over a pressure cooker and I touched it and the whole thing blew up in my face. That was quite a horrible experience. I spent three months in the same hospital where I worked. In the hospital, they took care of me beautifully. I was something to look at. If not for my mother-in-law, I would have been scarred for life. She was with me at that moment, and she immediately beat up a few eggs and smeared them all over my face. She did not have time to separate the yolks from the whites. My chest was also burned which I only realized later, after I got undressed. My mother-in-law's first aid really saved me because I only had a few scars. The doctors were curious about who helped me because they were impressed with her first aid.

I remember lying in bed and crying at my misfortune; my face was horrible to look at. It was so bad that my friend, Sheinele Koton, who was pregnant, didn't want to come to see me so she shouldn't be shocked and lose the baby. Liova saw me and said: "Why are you crying? You are already married." I looked at myself in the mirror and couldn't recognize myself. For months, I kept finding skin peeling off.

In the meantime, we decided that we wanted to start a family. I wanted a child so much but when I did not get pregnant for a long time I began to worry about whether I could bear a child after all the war traumas.

Meanwhile, many other people started leaving the DP camp. The ones who had good connections outside left the earliest, like our friends Ester and Hirshel Kagan. They were sent an affidavit by the Bund organization in the U.S. Henny Aronson and her husband, Folia, met his brother in Austria. He was a soldier in the U.S. Army. When the brother returned to the U.S. he immediately made them an affidavit to immigrate. They were the first ones to go to the U.S. We had no place to go yet. Many tried to convince us that we should go to Israel. Representatives from the Jewish Agency came knocking on the door in the middle of the night to convince survivors to go to Israel. This was during the time of the illegal immigration [mapilim] to Palestine [before independence in May 1948]. Mostly they took the youngsters. Ironically, those same people eventually immigrated to the U.S.

At some point, we all decided that we would immigrate to Israel. In 1948 Nechama went to Israel even though she received an affidavit to go to the U.S. She left Germany with her good friend, Reva. They were the first to leave. We packed them up with whatever we had. I gave her a few dollars and a pot, some clothes, and they left. I didn't tell them I was pregnant.

It took a long time to travel to Israel and then they went straight into the army in the newly formed State of Israel. This was just before Israel gained independence. I remember listening on the radio in 1948. Everyone was very excited. I have a photo of us listening to the radio. We believed that Israel would be a place where we could finally live in peace as Jews.

The Sidrer parents decided that they couldn't let the girls go alone so Feival and Chaya decided to go to Israel too. During those years in Landsberg, Feival was working as an electrician so he had saved a bit of money. Thus, they could buy airline tickets. At that time, you could fly but you could not take much luggage, therefore, I remember Chaya putting on five dresses under her coat—she looked like a barrel. They prepared a shipment to send to Israel and bought a refrigerator and sewing machine. I had a set of dishes for six, and a few other odds and ends, including the famous accordion. This was the accordion which Liova bought. He knew how to play because he had studied piano as a child. They eventually gave the accordion to Nechama and she has kept it all these years. She gave that accordion to Ettie.

It was at this time that I learned that I was pregnant. Hallelujah. I felt good during my pregnancy and continued working in the hospital. Just before Liova's parents left for the newly established State of Israel we told them that I was pregnant. We agreed that we would wait until the baby was born and we would follow. After they left, we moved into their apartment because it was bigger than ours.

One day, I invited my friend, Mara, for a Sabbath *cholent* [typical Jewish Sabbath stew]. Liova finished the meal and left to meet someone. I was cleaning the pot and enjoying my friend's company when suddenly I got terrible stomach cramps; my stomach was killing me. I thought that the *cholent* had given me cramps. I did not expect this. My neighbor was a religious woman and I asked her: "I have pain in my stomach; I thought it would be in my back." She said: "Of course it can be the pain [of childbirth]." According to my calculation it was too soon to give birth, but I soon realized what was happening. My doctor, a German professor, told me to go to the hospital in my eighth month.

I sent Mara to find Liova, but he was nowhere to be found. She went to the motor pool where he worked and they sent an ambulance to pick me up to take me to the hospital in the center of Landsberg. Munich hospital was too far. This was the St. Martin hospital which is next to the Lech River in the old section of the city. It was run by nuns and had crucifixes hanging above each bed. They took me in without any questions, straight into the delivery room. They told me to walk around the room; I walked back and forth in terrible pain. The nurse took me in and called the doctor but it was too late; the baby was coming too quickly. The nurse delivered me and told me to push. I pushed so hard that I broke blood vessels in my face. That's what happens when you don't have a doctor. Eventually, the doctor arrived and delivered the baby.

Our daughter Ettie was born on April 23, 1949. It was a wonderful moment for me. I stayed in the hospital with all the crucifixes for one week. I was torn to pieces from the birth, but it was okay, this was part of the deal. I was proud of my baby's birth and coincidentally, the Prince of England, Charles, was born a few days later [actually, he was born six months earlier]. I was always hungry like a wolf so I asked Liova to bring me food. A friend cooked a chicken for me and sent it to the hospital.

When I arrived home from the hospital, I had nothing for a baby. I had no crib, no diapers. I had a few sheets and tore them into diapers. A neighbor gave me undershirts from her child. According to Jewish tradition, you never prepare for a baby in advance, as this would incur the *Ein ha Ra* [evil eye]. I accumulated some things, but not enough, so every day I had to boil diapers on the *primus* [a small burner used for cooking]. I nursed the baby and I had plenty of milk. She was beautiful and gained weight. Do you know what it was like for me to become a mother? It was great. I named her after my mother, Eta. We called her Etale. I was in heaven.

We sent a telegram to the family in Israel that a baby girl was born. My mother-in-law wrote that we should not come yet to Israel—wait! There was a war, fighting and shortage of food. In the meantime, we heard that the U.S. was opening the doors to more immigrants. We registered for a visa and decided to let fate take its course. We had to prepare so many documents for this application. We had to find a Rabbi to get some certificate of marriage. We also had no birth certificates. We had to return to Munich many times for interviews. We didn't know if we would be accepted.

We waited and waited and suddenly, in May [April] 1950, we got the papers to go to the U.S., including papers for the new baby. Why did this process take so long? The government did not want to pay for the trip so they looked for families to sponsor our trip. Eventually, the HIAS (Hebrew Immigrant Aid Society) helped us and paid for our ticket. We did not mention that we had relatives in the U.S. because we didn't want any help from them. We wanted to be independent because we had heard lots of stories about families who rejected surviving relatives. We were not sure which members of our family wanted us or which ones said what—it did not bother us. Some said: "We'll get the family together," some said: "No." Many years later, we eventually met some members of our families in the U.S. and we learned that some were, indeed, afraid of being burdened with refugees.

We were told that we were leaving on May 2, 1950. We sent a telegram to the Sidrers in Israel that we were going to the U.S. They wished us well and we prepared ourselves to leave. In Landsberg many drivers from the motor pool where Liova worked came to say goodbye to him. They loved him. Just before we left Germany, I went to visit the Dachau concentration camp site, a 40-minute ride from Landsberg. There is a monument on the mass grave. I went to the spot and said goodbye to my father.

EN ROUTE TO AMERICA

We traveled to Munich and from there to Bremen. In Bremen there were barracks of people waiting for the ship. This is where Ettie started walking. We stayed for four days. We would go into the city and walk around. We had very little money. We bought lemons and oranges to take with us in case of seasickness on the boat.

We left [from Bremerhaven, Germany] on the *USS General C.C. Ballou*, which was a U.S. military transport ship. It was definitely not the *Queen Mary*. Because I was travelling with a child, they gave me a cabin to share with another woman and her child. The men had a hammock to sleep in at the bottom of the ship.

They fed us the best food imaginable; it was outstanding, but I was as sick as a dog. I could not even go to eat in the dining room which was beautifully set with white linens and fine dishes. The food was wonderful and Ettie ate everything; she wasn't sick for a minute. But anything I ate, I vomited everything. The captain told me to eat, even if I felt sick. "You must keep your stomach full," so I always did what the captain said. I ate and ate and threw up and ate again. Papa [Liova] didn't have any seasickness at all. The trip did not cost us, so we didn't have anything to complain about. We had some bad weather. I remember seeing flying or jumping fish.

The rest of the time I was on the deck walking with the baby. I put her in a harness while we were up on deck so she shouldn't fall. The trip took nine days. Liova used to come up to visit every once in a while. He worked on the ship cleaning toilets but still had a lot of free time. He would spend many hours playing chess with the men downstairs. He wasn't sick for a minute. I got angry and told him to come and spend some time with his baby.

We reached New York harbor on a Saturday night, May 15, 1950 [the USS General Baloo, arrived Sunday, May 14, 1950]. The boat docked way out in the harbor the first night, not at the pier. No one slept that night; we all remained on deck and stared at the Statue of Liberty. I left the baby sleeping in the cabin. Some were jumping, crying, singing, dancing. I did not cry, jump or sing. I could only think to myself, What will happen to us now? We do not know a soul in the city. Where will we go, what do we do, how do we begin this next chapter? We decided, that if we came this far, we would see what happens, like everything else.

MAMA'S PUBLIC INTERVIEWS

Mom never went public with interviews, as did others for some of the major testimonial projects over the years. When we asked her direct questions, she would answer and tell us bits and pieces of her story. We finally got the entire story on CDs, which have been transcribed herein. However, in her later years, she gave interviews to high school students, presentations to her co-residents at the senior center in Kadima, Israel, and speeches at the Lithuanian Association gatherings.

Once, when Mom was visiting me and my family in Barcelona, Spain, she agreed to answer some questions for a young high school student. Why this student? And why in Barcelona? I was working in Barcelona and my husband, Jacob, was a member of the Rotary club. A daughter of a Rotary member learned that we were Jewish and Israeli and she wanted to speak to us about the Holocaust. When we told her that my mother, a survivor, was currently visiting us, she could not believe her luck and was excited to be able to get a first-hand account for her school project. These are her questions and Mom's responses.

1. What gave you strength to carry on fighting for survival?

a) Friendship was extremely important. I was all alone in the camp. One day when we were lined up for roll call, I found myself standing next to four other girls/women because our registration numbers were similar. It was Henny, Tanya, Rochele, Yocheved and me. Three were much older and were nurses and Henny was my age. We decided to stay together. We shared everything and took care of each other. We shared food and we slept in the same bunk. We even shared the brown water—supposedly coffee—so we could wash our hair ... we were afraid of getting lice.

b) Another important factor for survival was a sense of humor. Henny had the best sense of humor. We had wooden bunks where we slept together on straw. We slept close together to stay warm and would joke at night about the things we dreamed about for the future. We dreamed of survival in order to be able to buy a loaf of bread and eat as much as we wanted. We used to dream and laugh about eating a loaf of bread, listening to Russian music and smoking American cigarettes.

c) We also wanted to survive in order to find our families. We had no knowledge of anyone in the family and we had no idea who was alive. I never found out until after liberation when I was found by my father-in-law.

d) I always believed that work would help me survive. I was young and strong and could work but I always remembered my father's words: "Never volunteer for anything." This proved to be right and kept me alive.

e) We focused on survival by trying to keep ourselves clean at every chance we had. We had a fear of lice because we believed that they brought disease. One winter we were near a frozen stream, we broke the ice and washed ourselves. We never got sick. Luckily, we never got our periods during these years. I never can remember a moment when I thought of giving up ... not even once.

2. Was it difficult to continue with the life lived before?

Most survivors were roaming around Europe searching for family members or stories about where they were last seen or other information about their fate. I also started searching for my family. Some thought that they could find family members by going back to their cities and towns and some did go back. Many found out that no one else survived.

By word of mouth we heard of the Displaced Persons camps that were established around Europe and many started travelling to these camps. These camps posted lists of names and everyone shared knowledge and information about others. Surviving Jews were wandering around and every new person who came into a town or village was questioned and the information was registered or just passed on verbally.

3. Did you notice a big change in your personality after the war?

Yes. I stopped believing in any religious laws. I stopped believing in God. I wasn't afraid of anything. We went to the U.S. without knowing English and with a baby (Ettie). The war experiences made me grow up fast. I was 16 when the war broke out. Such experiences make you an adult. I wanted a lot of children. If we would have had more money, I would have had more children. I never wanted to go to work and leave my children to be raised by someone else.

My husband and I knew each other for a very short time in the ghetto during the war. We got married after a short courtship. I really did not know him very well. After the war he wanted to do everything … learn to fly, amateur radio was an obsession for him. He also grew up quickly. He worked many jobs in the U.S. in order to make a living.

4. Did telling the story make you feel better? What do you think happens to those people who don't talk about their experience in the camp?

No! Every time I tell the story it brings back the awful memories. I don't mind talking about it now but it does not make me feel better. You get upset when you tell the story. When you are upset you are afraid that you might not tell it correctly. For example, some people have been interviewed on tape for TV. Sometimes, if they were very young during the war, they make mistakes; they think they remember clearly; sometimes the fantasies become the memories.

I told my children the story, but I have friends who never told their children about it. I think that is wrong. If you do not tell the story the children don't know anything about you and your history. Many immigrant survivors wanted to Americanize themselves and therefore did not tell the story. I think this causes a loss of identity for your kids. Every single year I go to the memorials to the Holocaust, whether in the U.S. or Israel. I never missed one. Many of my acquaintances have stopped going, they don't bother anymore. I feel it is my obligation to attend.

5. What would you do if you had to live in the camp once more? Would you survive that horror?

I would probably commit suicide, but I never thought of this before.

In 2010 and 2011, Mama told her story to high school students at an international school in Israel for a "Living History Day" project. Students quoted her saying: "It was a fight for survival; you don't give up." And: "Every survivor is a fighter." Yes, Mama was a fighter!

PART II

TRAVELS IN MAMA'S FOOTSTEPS: MY ODYSSEY TO LITHUANIA AND POLAND

INTRODUCTION

The catalyst for this unprecedented trip back into my family's history came from the juxtaposition of various events. First, I was deeply involved in finalizing the text of Mama's autobiography. It had taken more time than expected because of my determination in finding additional sources to confirm all of Mama's facts. I wanted the facts to prove that her memories were correct, so no one could deny what she, her family and the European Jews suffered.

Secondly, I discovered the book *The Extermination of Jews in Stutthof Concentration Camp* by Danuta Drywa, which was published by the Stutthof State Museum in 2004. Fortuitously, it was Steven Aronson who showed me this book in his home library in Costa Rica. He had bought it directly from the Stutthof Museum on a previous visit. Steven is Henny Aronson's son; Henny and my mother were soul sisters and mutual saviors throughout the Stutthof ordeal and beyond. Steven and I were childhood friends through our mothers' incredibly strong bonds of love and friendship.

In addition to the details about the incarceration and suffering of Jewish inmates of the camp and its satellites, the Drywa book included maps of all the towns along what the Poles called the "Evacuation Routes"—better known to the prisoners as the death march. In her testimony, Mama could not remember the names of the towns along the route, except the first one, Praust, and the last one, from where she was liberated—Chinov (Yiddish pronunciations). I found Praust (Pruszcz) on the map, but the location of Chinov eluded me for years because I could not identify the correct Polish name to find it on any map, and I had no idea of the direction they were taken. Suddenly, before my eyes was the route marched by my mother with her little group of friends, in a column of thousands—in the minus 20 degrees centigrade (minus 4 degrees fahrenheit) Polish winter of January-March 1945. It also showed the route of various other death marches, including the one endured by my grandmother Chaya Sidrer, together with my aunts, Reva Sidrer and Nechama Santocki—but in a different direction.

At that moment, I had a visceral reaction and felt a strong need to see it for myself. I felt drawn to travel to the locations of her love stories, her suffering and her incredible strength. I originally thought that perhaps I would walk the entire 124 kilometer (77 mile) route, but decided against it. When I mentioned my desire to take a trip according to this map, Steven said he would join me, as he had never seen this portion of our mothers' shared journey. So, the idea was planted and the wheels were set in motion—but not by walking.

Almost as if on cue, or divinely ordained, the finances were acquired for this three-week odyssey. The application process to receive "Ghetto Pension Funds," for the slave labor my mother endured during the years in the Kovno ghetto, had begun two years earlier. These funds from the German government were earmarked for my mother while she was still alive. Unfortunately, she did not live to receive these monies, but they were available to her descendants. Suddenly, these funds appeared in my bank account. Thus, I started making concrete plans for my trip to Lithuania and Poland —'in Mama's footsteps.'

I must say, however, that throughout the preparations I was very nervous. Not of travelling alone—I was accustomed to that. I was nervous because I was travelling without Mom's blessing. She never, ever wanted to return to this bloody land, and she did not want anyone else in her family to do so. So, I rationalized to myself that the pension money was the sign of her authorization.

I attacked this trip like an army mission with a calendar, schedule and a strategic plan of everything I wanted to see, experience, and find. I carefully combed through Mom's story and dutifully recorded in a spreadsheet all the places, sites and 'artifacts' that she mentioned. I sent the plan to my guides to begin some of the research and preparations in advance. While not travelled in this order, the following are my descriptions and reflections from the trip.

LITHUANIA

My childhood was filled with stories about my parents' lives before, during and after the war. The holiest of the artifacts that my parents accumulated after the war were family photos. Since everything was lost during the war years, my mother engaged in extraordinary efforts to retrieve family photos from relatives around the world. She knew that many photos were exchanged between her family in Kovno and relatives in North and South America, South Africa, and Palestine. She succeeded in collecting these images and always displayed them on the wall in every one of her homes, in the U.S., Canada and Israel. Thus, I was familiar with the faces of those who survived and particularly of those who did not.

In addition to these images, at some time, my parents acquired a portfolio of reproduced drawings entitled *A Living Witness* by the Latvian artist, Ester Lurie.[1] She, too, was imprisoned in the Kovno ghetto and after the war drew what she had seen and what she remembered. These drawings were my first images of "the ghetto." In my mind, these were the only images of my parents' youth ... and I memorized each one. Just like the stories I heard about proms or sports events enjoyed by the parents of my American friends, these were my parents' version of their youth. My parents' narratives included anecdotes of daily survival, hunger, revolutionary activities, *Aktsias*, slave labor, the liquidation of the ghetto, the march to the trains and the horrible death of my aunt, Ida, who was incinerated in the *malina* during her attempt to hide, and more.

Reminiscent of one scene from the movie *The Pianist*, Papa told me that he saw the burning of the ghetto from his hiding spot across the river. He said: "When the ghetto was evacuated and liquidated I heard the screams and commotion from within." After the liberation by the Russians, on August 1, 1944, he immediately went to see the aftermath. Joined by others who also came out of hiding, together they buried the remains of those killed by the bombs or the fire. He said: "I cautiously came out of hiding and went back to my old house. A Lithuanian family was living there. They were shocked to see me alive, but since the war was almost over, it was senseless to get killed over property."

I felt it imperative to see the locations with my own eyes. After all, don't most kids want their parents to show them the "old neighborhood?" It was important for me to stand on the streets where my ancestors suffered, walked, tiptoed, marched, hid, slaved, feared, loved, married, escaped, survived—or died.

Mentioning "slaved," I must interject an anecdote, which seems a bit ludicrous to my sisters and me. If it weren't describing such a tragic event, it would possibly be worthy of a dark comedy skit. In applying for these "Ghetto Pension Funds" for our survivor parents, we were informed that the German government distinguishes between "forced" and "free will" labor during the ghetto years. How interesting!

We were informed that since, in past records, my father indicated that his work in the ghetto was "forced," and that he received some food for this work, he was denied the pension. Since my mother's work was designated as "free will" labor, she was eligible for monies from the fund. Of course, the semantics are absurd. None of the inmates, forced into and locked up in the Kovno ghetto (designated as a concentration camp in 1942) were laboring through "free will." They were forced to labor in order to survive. They were all imprisoned and feared for their lives, thus, how could it be declared free will? I relayed our sentiments about the semantics, and received a convoluted and incomprehensible explanation, which was almost humorous. Thus, we received the monies for Mama's "free will" labor, but not for Papa's "forced" labor. These funds helped me pay for my trip to Lithuania and Poland.

Kovno Ghetto The ghetto was created by the Germans in 1941 by encircling a large section of the town of Slabodka with barbed wire fences, guard posts and locked gates. Orders were posted that by August 15, 1941 all Jews had to be moved into the ghetto. As I drove across the bridge from Kaunas city center to Slabodka, I got a strange feeling in my gut. I am not sure whether it was fear or familiarity. Within a few minutes we were in front of the ghetto memorial stone.

We drove around the streets with an old map of the original ghetto streets, but, alas, the ghetto addresses I brought with me were no longer in existence or had been changed. After the liquidation of the ghetto, a huge part of the ghetto was bombed and burned down. It was a huge conflagration. This was the moment that my mother's sister, Ida, was killed during the burning of her hideout. Papa confirmed her death when he returned to the ghetto after his liberation and saw the death and destruction.[2]

Despite not finding their streets or homes, I did get a feeling for what the houses looked like and where the barbed wire fences might have been. I saw the cobblestone streets and wooden houses, central *Appel* (lineup) square (Democratu), the site of the vegetable gardens alongside the riverbank, the bridge connecting Slabodka to Kovno, and the road that led upwards toward the Ninth Fort, like in my grandfather's drawing.

Ironically, as a typical tourist, I found myself making mental comparisons between the three major ghettos I visited on this trip: Vilna, Krakow and Kovno. As far as ghettos go, Kovno ghetto was the most, how shall I say it, poor and decrepit. The Vilna and Krakow ghettos had buildings made of brick and were two or three stories high. The streets all had sidewalks, while the Kovno ghetto was in a poor and miserable-looking section, with small, shabby one or two-storey wooden houses, very few sidewalks and many potholes.

Stop this! I chided myself. Indeed, throughout the trip I was consumed by conflicting feelings. On the one hand, I am an avid traveler, amateur anthropologist and passionate tourist and was enjoying the architecture, art, culture, food, progress, roads, technology, landscapes—and shopping. But on a number of occasions I had to reprimand and remind myself of the major mission—I was not there to enjoy the sights—I came to record the past life and difficult times of our parents. I continually tried to manage both.

Interestingly, the question asked most often by friends and family during the trip and during formal and informal presentations was "How did you manage your emotions?" I wondered about that too. Throughout the three weeks, there were only a few crisis moments, but lots of gut-wrenching feelings and sorrow. For the most part, I felt almost like a journalist recording a story. Perhaps that's how I kept my guts in check.

Slabodka (Viliampole) I wanted to see my grandfather, Feival's, metal foundry on the corner of Kampas Kedaiiniy ir Vilkijos gatviy. We did find it, but it had been expanded and now manufactures a quality sports clothing line. *Zeide* built this site and invested all his own monies into the construction and new equipment ordered from abroad. In addition, his family lived in an apartment upstairs. However, when the Russians occupied Kovno in 1940, they nationalized all businesses and ousted the Sidrer family from their home, their life investment and their livelihood. Fortunately, or unfortunately, their fears of deportation to Siberia were unfounded.

Almost penniless, they had to find another place to live. My aunt, Reva, remembered the address, Kalnyechu Gatwe #15, and told me that it was a two-storey wooden building in Zaliakalnis. While the numbers have changed, I believe that the photo I took was, indeed, of the original house. From the window of this house, Reva witnessed the Lithuanian Auxiliary Forces, with their white armbands, fully armed, exiting the house across the street, to begin their massacre of Jews—before the Germans even entered the city.

My father recounted his thoughts and actions directly after his liberation on August 1, 1944: "I cautiously came out of hiding and went back to my old house. A Lithuanian family was living there. They were shocked to see me alive, but since the war was almost over, it was senseless to get killed over property." And that was the end of that dream.

As a declaration of full disclosure, in the back of my mind, I wondered if we had any rights to the foundry property. I had proof of ownership from the factory letterhead and from the futile communications between the Lithuanian Consul in Exile in New York and the Sidrer-Baran families from the 1950s and 1960s. And, in the Kaunas Archives, I was pleasantly surprised to find numerous tax audits, all signed by my grandfather, "Feivus Sidreris." However, my dreams of remuneration were shattered after communicating with a Lithuanian lawyer in Vilnius. She informed me that since I was not a Lithuanian citizen and it was already after 1999, I had no rights to property or remuneration. That was the end of this dream too.

The Ninth Fort-Viliampole It was important for me to visit the infamous Ninth Fort for a few reasons. First, this was the site of mass murder of Jews, not only from Lithuania, but also from Germany and France. From November 1941 to June 1944, around 45,000 Jews—adults and children—were murdered at this site, including my great grandmother, Ester Liba Disner, and other family members.

I recall being aware of the Ninth Fort since childhood—prior to the details that I learned from later research. My parents had close friends living in eastern Canada, Berel and Rochele Gempel. For a few years at Christmas time, we would get together in New York, or in Moncton, New Brunswick. I recall the adults getting seriously drunk while telling their war stories. One of those famous stories, which has been described in many historical accounts, in Mom's memoir, and by his own testimony, was Berel's escape from the Ninth Fort on Christmas Eve 1943, along with 64 other *Sonderkommando* slave-prisoners. I remember listening from my bedroom, as they recounted the stories and celebrated that escape in 1943, their escape together out of Soviet-occupied Kovno in 1946, and their survival—with laughter, songs, tears and lots and lots of vodka.

And, of course, I always remember the drawing rendered by my *zeide* (grandfather), Feival, of the Jews being marched up the hill from the ghetto to the Ninth Fort after the big *Aktsia* in October 1941. The people faced an uphill climb of over 2 kilometers before they were murdered at the fort. Indeed, during my visit, I wanted to see that same view that had been immortalized by my *zeide*. But it was summer, and the road uphill was covered by big trees and new housing—so it was a totally different scene. My guide, Simonas, was impressed with the drawing.

Raudondvaris Just before the liquidation of the ghetto in June 1944, my father answered the call for volunteers to fix the trucks and jeeps of the Germans before their rushed retreat to the west, as the Russians were approaching from the east. Together with a few other mechanics, they made plans for an escape.

In Papa's words (1987): "The Nazis had to have some jeeps repaired in a garage outside the barbed wire fence. I knew I was to be taken out by car and I planned to escape. When the guard was at the far end of the garage, I climbed over an incredibly high fence, after disconnecting all the jeeps' cables and puncturing the tires."

It was only just before my trip that my 89-year-old aunt, Reva Baran, told me the name of the location to which he was taken and from which he escaped. The German vehicles were housed in an estate with a big wall around the perimeter, a few kilometers from the ghetto in Slabodka. The name of this place is Raudondvaris, which means 'red mansion' in Lithuanian.

I wanted to see with my own eyes the site of the stories of his miraculous escape from the Germans and the route he took into hiding. Papa told me (1987): "I ran until I got to a flour mill near my father's factory [Slabodka/Viliampole]. A peasant woman who had once worked for my father, and was indebted to him for his help in paying her son's tuition, found me hiding there and gave me food. At one point she was afraid to keep me hidden any longer and I left and found a hiding place with a woman who lived directly across the street from the ghetto."

I naively thought I would be able to see the "famous" fence that he scaled to get out of the compound and the wheat fields in which he hid. Indeed, I went to Raudondvaris, which, in its newly renovated condition, is truly a magnificent estate and a major tourist attraction. Needless to say, I was unable to see any fences or wheat fields because the site is completely surrounded by a new red brick wall and the fields outside its perimeter have luxury villas for many who commute to work in Kaunas.

I crossed the bridge from Slabodka into Kovno, just like Papa did, but I was driving in a car, while he walked; I was not afraid, but I am sure he feared for his life as he nonchalantly crossed the bridge in broad daylight, in direct view of an German soldier. As I recall the story, he even had the *chutzpah* to ask the soldier for a light for his cigarette.

Kovno City Since childhood, I recall my mother telling me about Kovno and the beautiful tree-lined boulevard Laisves Aleja, where she would meet up and walk with her friends. The boulevard was at the base of the Zaliakalnis hill, which is the neighborhood where the Santocki family lived.

I specifically booked a hotel on the Laisves Aleja, because of its centrality and because it was Mom's favorite street. This boulevard housed all the upscale shops, restaurants and cafes, many which were owned or run by Jews before the war. Even today, the street is high-end and displays the best in designer items, hotels, coffee shops, restaurants—and money changers.

The Sidrer family also has history on this boulevard, as we are linked to the construction of the magnificent modernist post office, right on the intersection of the Laisves Aleja and Kanto Gatwe. It was built between 1930-1931, during the architectural boom throughout the country. The internal design and decorations were also well known for their modernist beauty. The one who did all the electrical work for the building was my grandfather, Feival Sidreris (the Lithuanian ending -is indicates a man's name). There is a bronze plaque in the lobby with his name on it, together with those of the other craftsmen and construction workers involved in the project. Zeide was responsible for all the electrical work in the building. This was my *zeide*'s profession before he started his metal foundry. It was eery to see his name on the plaque.

I was so fortunate that my aunt Reva, who at the age of 89 still has a sharp memory, was able to give me the addresses of her family homes in Kovno. I found the building housing their first apartment on Poshkosh Gatwe 14, their second home above the factory in Viliampole, and then their last home in Zaliakalnis, at Kalnyechu Gatwe 15, where they lived after being evicted by the Russians.

The building which houses the Kaunas National Archive is like something out of an old Soviet movie. We walked up the irregular stairs to the third floor of an old white building with dying plants in the staircase, conveniently located in an inner courtyard off the Laisvis Aleja, across from my hotel. This building was built on the site of the old Maironio Street synagogue, which was demolished. We entered a room lined with shelves and four computers, desks, and chairs. The lady supervisor, in true form, was whispering as she informed us how to use the archive. She kept 'shushing' us, which made me laugh, as I was reminded of the many librarians I had known in the past. The archives allowed me a glimpse into my family's past and offered a few surprises.

In my original plan I naively fantasized about marching into my mother's high school, Gymnasium #3, introducing myself and requesting to see my mother's school records. However, that fantasy ended when my guide informed me that the school building had been converted into apartments. Luckily, I learned that the school records had been transferred to the National Archive. So the search began for Zlata Santockyte's file (the ending –yte in Lithuanian indicates an unmarried woman). And we found it in the form of three documents: a letter handwritten by my grandfather, requesting admissions, a birth certificate and an official transcript of her grades from primary school. What a feeling! What a find!

Then my guide informed me that there was another file on a girl named Fruma Santockyte. I almost dismissed it as a coincidence; there was no Fruma in my mother's history, I thought. However, upon closer observation, the letter, written one year after the request for Zlata, was signed by Eta Santockiene, my grandmother. It suddenly became evident that this was my aunt Ida's application and transcript for admissions—she was two years younger than my mother—and, lo and behold, her official name was Fruma! It is possible that she was named after my great-great grandmother, who was possibly "Fruma" Sara, but at home she was called Ida. My mother never mentioned this and I wonder if she even knew her official name, because she recorded her sister's death in the "Pages of Testimony" in Yad Vashem's database as Ida Santocki.

From the handwriting in the letter, it looked like my grandmother had someone else, perhaps her daughter Ida, write the text of the letter and that she then signed her name. Was she illiterate or was she insecure about her language skills? Suddenly, I had a flashback and remembered doing exactly the same for my mother—she would ask me to write official letters for her, and then she would sign them! My mother was literate in five languages, but I think she was insecure about the quality of her writing for official purposes. I can identify.

Searching for the name Sidreris led to five files of tax audits from my grandfather's metal foundry in Viliampole. The audits showed all the expenses, salaries, names of employees and revenue.

All citizens and residents of many Eastern European countries had to be registered. If they wished to move from one town to another, they needed what is called an "internal passport," which is an identity card. I found one for my grandfather Santocki's sister, Berta Blatiene, who was murdered at the Ninth Fort. I also found such documents for my Sidrer grandparents, Chaya and Feival. They all looked so young.

Zaliakalnis The section of Kovno/Kaunas called Zaliakalnis was referred to in Yiddish as *Auf dem Grinem Barg* (On the Green Hill). One of the hallmarks of this neighborhood on the hill is the funicular railway, constructed in 1931, which transported residents from the city center to the top. I recall my mother mentioning that she travelled on it, and so did I. It was a very short ride and cost about 10 cents.

In the archives I found a request to modify the Santocki house at 33 Kapsu Gatwe. It included the floor plans submitted by the owner. Thus, I realized that the house did not belong to my grandparents. I should have realized it because my mother never mentioned any attempt to get compensation for their home *cum* butcher shop after the war.

My mother lived with her family in this rented house. My guide, Simonas, acquired a pre-war map of the street lots and house numbers. Kapsu street runs the length of Zaliakalnis. I was advised by Simonas that the numbers of the houses on the streets had been changed after the war. According to the map, it seems that the house which today is numbered 59 Kapsu Gatwe might be the same one that was numbered 33 before the war. There was even another house behind it, number 59A. This might have been the house of the Russian neighbor who housed Mama after her return to Kovno in 1945. It was this neighbor who returned the family photo to Mom, all wrinkled up, because it had been hidden in the straw mattress of a bed. To my mother, this was the most precious gift in the world. And, despite the fact that this neighbor appropriated their home and possessions, Mama was grateful that they housed and fed her after the war.

As we stood on the sidewalk gesturing and speaking in English, a man came toward us with an unfriendly, questioning look on his face. I became physically uncomfortable, remembering my parents' mantra after the war—"it was not worth getting killed for property." Despite all these clues, it was impossible to declare with absolute certainty that the house I saw was, indeed, Mom's childhood home —but, it fit Mama's description and fits the floor plans too, so, in my mind, I decided that it was.

The Seventh Fort-Zaliakalnis My mother described her family's unsuccessful attempt to flee Kovno after the Germans started bombing the airport on that life-altering Saturday evening, June 21, 1941. She lost track of time, but after about one week of walking among masses of refugees they were eventually turned back to Kovno. They were arrested and forced into the Seventh Fort, one of the nine forts surrounding the city, built at the end of the 19th century by the Czars to protect Kovno. Here, the women and children were separated from the men, but had to watch the men being marched to the fields outside the fort and listen to the massacre of almost 3,000 men. This particular fort happened to be very close to their home in Zaliakalnis. But later, the women and children were taken to the Ninth Fort and eventually released. The distance between the Ninth Fort and their home in Zaliakalnis is approximately 5 kilometers; they had to walk home weak, tired, hungry, and grieving, convinced that their father/husband had been murdered.

The story of the capture, arrest and incarceration of her family is described in detail in Mama's memoir, and in various other sources. But the most poignant and fateful story of this chapter in their lives was how my grandfather, Yakov Santocki, avoided being shot along with the other thousands of Jewish male prisoners. Just after he finished digging at the pit, and after he was instructed to undress and remove his boots, he boldly told the Lithuanian pointing a gun at him that he was about to kill a *Savanoris*. He showed the Lithuanian youth the medal he received in recognition of his voluntary military service to their country. He proudly kept this medal in his pocket at all times; the Lithuanian pulled him out of the killing lineup and told him to wait in another part of the fort. That medal saved his life.[3] Thus, the medal was indirectly responsible for the well-being and survival of the family during the three difficult ghetto years, and possibly thereafter.

I can remember this story since childhood and I wanted to find this famous *Savanoris* medal and reinstate it to our family. I sent Simonas, my guide, an Internet image of the medal and asked him if he knew any antique dealers. Indeed, he had a colleague who dealt in antiques. During my visit, this dealer brought me a *Savanoris* medal, for which I gladly paid his price. Was this *Zeide* Yakov's actual medal? We will never know, but, for me it is. I just wish I could have shown it to Mama while she was still alive.

In addition to the excitement of acquiring the *Savanoris* medal, I was thrilled to find the official handwritten registration of my grandfather's military record in the National Archive in Vilnius. I now learned that Santockis, Jakubas, served in the 6th Battalion, Company #3, near Mariampole (which was near his home in Kalvarija). He was recruited on November 28, 1919 and transferred from one site to another. He was a Lithuanian patriot, but was killed because he was a Jew.

Sugihara House and Museum Forty years have passed since I first learned about Chiune Sugihara, the Japanese Consul to Lithuania. He was a true hero and humanitarian because he refused to stop writing *laissez-passer* visas for Polish refugees who escaped to Kovno after the Nazi conquest of Poland in 1939. Even when he was ordered by his government to leave the city, he continued signing visas at the train station before departure. He is credited for saving over 2,000 lives. For this, he was honored posthumously as a "Righteous Gentile" by the Government of Israel. Possibly as a result of these actions, he was dismissed from the foreign service after his return to Japan.

After first learning about Sugihara many years ago, I remember asking my mother why she did not go to get this visa. She said that the *Litvaks* (Lithuanian Jews) knew nothing about Sugihara or the visas; another one of those quirks of history. The consulate has been converted into a museum and attracts many visitors, including descendants of those 2,000 lucky souls. During my visit to the museum, two American women arrived, cousins, whose grandfathers were among those who received the life-saving visa from Sugihara. They were thrilled to find their ancestors' names on a list at the museum. It was an extremely moving visit for them and for me listening to their story.

My guide, Simonas, who is the Director of the Sugihara Museum, invited me to join his weekly Cabbalat Shabbat, held by his little Jewish community. Inside the large building, which is some sort of culinary school, the community rents a small basement room. There is a long table and the room has kitchen cabinets, a fridge and a sink. This is where they meet for their communal prayer and "dinner" each week. This little congregation included about 20 older souls—mostly men and a few women. To me, each seemed to be lonely, poor but happy to be celebrating together. I asked why they did not meet at the only remaining synagogue—the beautiful baroque-style Chor Synagogue. I was told that they do not like the man who is the *gabai* (manager) of the synagogue and refuse to have anything to do with him; so instead, they rent this basement room. One man took over the "proceedings," we made all the *brachot* (prayers) and sang all the verses of *Lecha Dodi* ... I was very impressed with how detached and controlled I had been throughout my trip, and then, right here, I lost it.

Simonas introduced me as a "Kovno girl" and I told them all the names of our Kovno family members. "Zivov? Of course, I know Zivov!" said one lady who knew my cousin, Grisha's deceased brother, the gynecologist; another man knew my great uncle Uriel

Zivov personally. Another guest knew Jay Ipson, a friend of my family. It was like a high school reunion. Some of these people were probably younger than me but they looked older. There were 35,000 Jews in Kovno before the war, and now there are only 150—most of them not originally from Kovno.

Fortuitously, my cousins Grisha and Sonia Zivov were vacationing in Kovno at the same time as I was there, and took me around the center of town to show me where they grew up. They immigrated to Israel and married there in 1972. The stories of my great uncle Uriel Zivov peppered the narrative. He migrated to Kovno after his banishment to Siberia by the Russians in 1940. His wife and two children were murdered by the Germans in Kalvarija. Grisha is one of the sons from his second marriage. Uriel served as the *gabbai* (warden) of the Chor Synagogue until he immigrated to Israel in 1987. He was my mother's favorite uncle and she maintained contact with him throughout the years and despite the fears.

Sidrer Family Homes Thankfully, my aunt Reva was able to remember the addresses of their homes in Kovno. Their first one was on Poshkosh Gatwe #14. I found the building and entered the huge arch to a green courtyard that was overrun with weeds. I found the door to their apartment according to her description. I wish I had the courage to knock on the door and view the interior, but I did not think it prudent. Their second home was upstairs in the metal foundry that Feival built in the suburb of Slabodka, across the river Neris. After the factory was nationalized and they were evicted by the Russians, they moved to their third home in Zaliakalnis, on Kalnyechu Gatwe #15.

Gestapo Headquarters, Secondary School and Train Station The building, which was commandeered for the Gestapo headquarters, is a huge beautiful structure stretching over a large portion of a block on Vytautus Prospekt at Gastucho Gatwe. I entered the magnificent lobby of this Nation's Cultural Center and once again I chided myself for admiring its enormous wide staircases and ceiling-to-floor modernist stained-glass windows. The beauty of the lobby decried its ugly history. Nevertheless, it was here in the kitchen that my grandfather worked throughout the ghetto years. And, just as Mama told us, two buildings away was her secondary school. I could now understand how she had a direct view from the window into her school courtyard when she was cleaning offices and toilets for the Gestapo. I empathized with her anger and anguish as she watched her classmates playing happily and freely in the yard while she was a prisoner.

The Kovno train station is another enormous, white building standing majestically at the very end of the wide Vytautus Prospekt that weaves through Kovno. According to my aunt, Reva, the prisoners who survived after the liquidation of the ghetto were marched to this station. They marched a distance of almost 5 kilometers, right through the center of Kovno, en route to Stutthof and Dachau concentration camps. She remembers it clearly: "We were marched from the ghetto in Slabodka across the bridge and through the city of Kovno to the train station." She also remembers the experience in the train cars: "There was one small window with barbed wire; we travelled for three days; there was hysteria, tears and poor Feival had diarrhea."

---

1. Lurie, 1958
2. Rapoport, p. 261
3. Zilber, 2017 November.

POLAND

Auschwitz-Birkenau Concentration Camps I booked myself on a tour bus to Auschwitz because it was the most direct and quick way to get there, visit and return. Of course, that meant that I sacrificed my independence and solitude for convenience and time, and could not be alone with my observations, my reflections or my sadness. The museum-ness of Auschwitz was a bit of an affront to my emotions, just as are the museums in Dachau and Stutthof. But I, if anyone, should understand the value of educating the world through visits to these "museums of genocide." Father Patrick Desbois said, after his unprecedented research on the innumerable killing fields of Eastern Europe, that Hitler made a huge mistake building concentration camps.[1] Why? Because they have become museums and shrines and people come to visit them. Until his monumental research, few came to visit the 1.5 million who were murdered and buried in unmarked pits. In the past, there were no shrines or markers. Today, some markers have been erected with dubious explanations.

To me, seeing the barracks, bathrooms and buildings in the camp was less upsetting than seeing the exhibits of mountains of shoes, eyeglasses, food containers, and suitcases. I would look at the shoes and wonder, was that my (little) aunt Genya's shoes or my name-sake-grandmother, Eta's, hairbrush? To my surprise, I learned that they were not murdered in Auschwitz per se, but actually in the sister camp nearby, Birkenau. The ubiquitous photo of train tracks entering through the front archway of a long and windowed building is of Birkenau. That image always reminds me of a face with a huge cavernous mouth swallowing the tracks and the human cargo which passed through its jowls.

I saw an old railroad car; I walked the tracks; I walked to the site of their disembarking and I walked as close as permissible to the location of the bombed-out gas chambers and crematoria. I learned that Eta and Genya were never processed; they never spent any amount of time in this camp. They were simply unloaded and marched to the final destination. I tried to imagine my grandmother's stoic and strong demeanor as she calmed her 11-year-old daughter as they walked hand in hand to their death with thousands of others.

And then, I walked a few more meters to four black marble slabs in front of a little "pond"—a memorial for the dead. This pond was not for aesthetics. No, it was here that they dumped the human ashes from the ovens. This was an unexpected kick to the gut. I decided that this was where I wanted to light my *Yorzeit* (remembrance) candles. But, lo and behold, as I started to set up the candles, the sky darkened and the wind kicked up with a gale force. My immediate response, as I smiled up to the sky was, "okay Mom, I got your message—but I had to come." I recited a shortened *Kaddish* (prayer for the dead), told them that they were not forgotten, and took a photo of their final resting place. The bus ride back to Krakow with the other tourists was heavy, as I nonchalantly mentioned to them that my family was murdered here.

Stutthof Concentration Camp Approximately 34 kilometers (22 miles) east of Gdansk is the town of Sztutowo. In German, the camp was called "Stutthof", the first Nazi concentration camp established on Polish soil. For me, this name is indelibly inscribed in my psyche and evokes a physical reaction. Steven Aronson (Henny's son) and I travelled by train and got off in front of the large concrete entrance sign.

We met with the archive director at the camp, who gave each of us a copy of the original registration forms with the prisoner numbers for our mothers, my grandmother and the two younger girls, Reva and Nechama. According to my aunt, Reva, "these numbers determined the work camp and ultimately determined the groups for evacuation." Indeed, Mama's number was 41410 and Henny's number was 42018.

Then we met Marcin Owsinski, Director of the Educational Department, who is collecting and publishing testimonials of survivors (a bit late, I thought). He showed us two books by Jewish prisoners that the museum has published. The purpose is to enhance and improve their educational programs at the museum. I was not sure my mother would approve of having her story published by them, but I was glad to hear that they are educating the public. Danuta Drywa's book, in which I discovered the "Evacuation Route" maps, was also published by the Stutthof Museum.

I learned that the first prisoners in Stutthof were political prisoners from Poland and numerous other nations. Jews were being killed or imprisoned in ghettos at first but only started flooding the camp from 1944; the Kovno women arrived in July 1944. In fact, at some point, they had to build additional barracks for the Jewish women. The barracks were not ready to receive the large numbers, but the women were housed there anyway—right in the birch-tree forest. I read somewhere that Stutthof was called "the most beautiful concentration camp." I didn't know there was a beauty competition. What an incomprehensible distinction!

On exhibit at the camp museum, I saw the striped uniform and the wooden clogs that were worn by all the prisoners. I got a knot in my stomach as I looked at the infamous examination table, where SS men would examine all the women and girls, regardless of age—

even internally. Henny (2009) described it as a "huge ping-pong type of table." My mother described that examination vividly.

Henny and Zlata probably did not spend much time at Stutthof proper after their original registration, intrusive internal body examinations and uniform distribution. There were dozens of satellite camps and it was possible that they were sent to work at various ones. According to Henny (1994), they slaved 13-14 hours a day and were taken by truck to work locations. Pruszcz (Praust) is the one that Mama described, specifically because she was here for her 20th birthday.

The Death March/Evacuation Route I was happy that I hired Michal Maj as our tour guide. In the email interview, I gave him a list of the towns through which I wanted to drive. He wrote back and asked if this was the "Stutthof Evacuation Route" as it is called in Poland. I wrote back indicating that 'we' called it the death march. He came prepared with printouts of his research; he had made himself an expert on the subject. He was an incredible asset. But he did remind us that the concentration camps were built by the Nazis on Polish soil, so we should not refer to them as "Polish concentration camps." Point taken.

Indeed, he was a walking encyclopedia! He was passionate about each subject and a perfectionist in ensuring that we hear everything he knows. He was devoted to helping us find all the known and unknown legs of our journey. It was he who found locations on Google Maps and guided us to the school and train station in Gdinya. It was he who helped us find the councillor of Rybno, who was responsible for the interpretative signs about the Evacuation Route in Chinov. And, of course, he was our translator and interpreter, so that we could make more intimate contact with local people. He quickly earned their trust so that they responded willingly to our questions.

Pruszcz to Chynowie We found the airfield in Pruszcz/Praust where Mom and Henny labored in this subcamp of Stutthof. We tried to imagine how they slaved in difficult conditions and where they slept. Mom said they slept in round tents. Many women prisoners worked at the military airfield or at a nearby sugar factory. There were also many sub-camps around Praust. The Germans actually outsourced the labor of the prisoners to various companies and agencies, which paid for this slave labor. This revenue went into the war effort.

Our guide found the blog of a Polish musician, named Marcin, whose passion and hobby is researching the history of the prisoners at Praust. We invited him for coffee to hear about his research. Marcin wants to save a hangar and the sugar factory as historical monuments. He uses hi-tech instruments to view artifacts beneath the surface. He has purchased documents from the UK and Denmark, which prove that the Germans were selling slave labor to specific companies.

He told us that the Germans had plans for Praust from before 1942. There were other available airfields but Hitler targeted Praust to design and test a new jet plane. Hitler thought this jet would help him win the war so he needed a big airfield. *Hitlerjugend* (youth) came here to learn to fly. There were also helicopters in the Praust airfield.

There are numerous memorials to the Pruszcz Evacuation. One monument was next to the airfield and a bunker where Marcin found human bones as he cleaned up the area. Another was in the center of town, near a supermarket and old church.

As the Russians gained momentum westward, the German military, SS and civilians started to retreat towards Germany. Instead of leaving the prisoners behind, the protocol throughout the Reich was to march the prisoners toward Germany. This event is known in Poland as the "Evacuation Route" and there are street signs, interpretive signs, cemeteries and memorials all along the 124 kilometer route. I was so impressed when I first learned about these commemorative symbols, until I realized that they were primarily commemorating the large number of Polish and foreign prisoners who were forced on this "evacuation" and not necessarily the Jewish ones.

My mother remembered only two dates with certainty during the death march: Pruszcz on February 5, 1945, because it was her 20th birthday, and Chinov/Chynowie on March 10, 1945, when they were liberated by the Russians. I recently learned that she actually began the death march from the Pruszcz sub-camp, at some time after February 5th. She could not remember the dates when she marched across the frozen Vistula River, or the towns in which they slept in barns, churches, or prisons. Thus, I photographed every barn, church and prison en route—could my mother have been here? Here? We travelled to each town according to the Drywa map: Cedry Wielki, Pruszcz, Pregngowo, Kolbude, Niestepowo, Zukowo, Prodkowo, Mlynek, Lebno, Luzino, Pszhowo and Chynowie.

The signs on the main road read "Ofiar Stutthof" (Stutthof victims' road). In almost every town and in each manicured churchyard and cemetery, we saw monuments to the Stutthof prisoners who died during the march. Some gravestones had lists of names of those buried in mass graves. All the names were Polish men; none were Jewish women. We could only assume that any Jewish corpses found along the route were collected and buried together with non-Jewish corpses. At one point the terrain began an uphill climb. If it was not enough that the prisoners suffered the coldest winter in 1945, walked in wooden clogs in the snow, wore only their pajama-uniforms and had maybe a blanket but no food ... they now had to walk uphill from Niestepowo. I could not imagine the agony of this march; I don't think anyone could.

At a farm house in Mlynek, we knocked on the door. A lady agreed to ask her elderly mother-in-law about prisoners coming through this road during the war. Yes, she remembered them.

At Luzino, we stopped at the firehouse and asked about the "Evacuation." They directed us to the church where the "evacuation prisoners" slept. We entered during mass and quietly viewed one mural on the arched beam depicting the death march from Stutthof and another about Auschwitz. A white marble sign and murals indicated that prisoners slept in this church during the march. I believe that Zlata and Henny might have been among those prisoners.

As per my mother's testimony, somewhere there was a town with a prison. While the town of Wehjerowo appeared on the map, it was not connected to one of the marked routes. And we never found any prison in any of the towns. We asked the councillor of Rybno/Chynowie, Andre J. Miedziak, if he knew of a town with a prison. He immediately identified Wehjerowo as the only possibility. We returned to this town and, indeed, found the prison and courthouse in the same courtyard. Bronze plaques identify this location as a site for "evacuation prisoners." We assume that the column came through this town and stayed in this prison—just like my mother described.

My mother's recollection of this episode was strong and the story was memorable because she vividly described the warmth of the prison, the attack of the body lice, and her elation at finding a pair of rubber boots to wear instead of the wooden clogs. She recalls that from this prison, she walked with her newly-found boots, and frozen toes, all the way to the town of Chinov/Chynowie. According to Henny, that walk lasted three days. In total, they were marched for 124 kilometers (77 miles).

The maps do not indicate that this town was part of the march. We believe that the German soldiers possibly made a decision to divert this column through Wehjerowo, perhaps because they knew there was a large facility for the prisoners to sleep in. I wrote to Danuta Drywa and she responded that mine was the first confirmation that a column of Jewish female prisoners had slept here before liberation. She was pleased to get this important account about the evacuation and the prison's history.

Chinov/Chynowie I remember the name of the town where my mother was liberated, as long as I remember myself. I felt a kind of trembling when we arrived and saw the interpretive signs about the "Evacuation from Stutthof." One described a temporary hospital/clinic that was set up in Leczyce. Others also gave testimony about this makeshift hospital.[2] This sounds like the town mentioned in Mom's testimony where one of her friends was cared for. It might also have been near the abandoned house they found, still with stocks of food, after liberation.

We spoke to a few elderly neighbors and people walking on the street and asked them if they could remember the prisoners during the war. The older residents recalled that there were three barns with prisoners. Mama recalled the "tremendous" barn and Henny said "there were big bales of hay like benches up to the ceiling ... that was a real Dante's Inferno, that was a real hell ... surrounded by death ... they closed the barn doors ... they poured gasoline all around ... the next thing we hear banging and Russian spoken." (Aronson, 1994) Because of the innumerable deaths in the barns, the residents never used the barns again and they fell into disrepair and collapsed; there is no sign of them now except for the foundations.

We met a mason walking home from work who proudly told us that he had worked on putting up the signs about the death march. We wanted more information about the numerous signs, so he directed us to a village official. This man was working on his garden and he gave us directions to the home of the Rybno town councilor. We knocked on the door of the *Radny* (councilor), Andrej Miedziak, and his wife told us that he was at a meeting in the town hall. We found him in the town hall in the middle of a dinner with some 25 people. Our guide explained who we were and he came out and hugged us as if we were long-lost relatives. All the villagers at this dinner were very welcoming; they were shocked that our mothers survived as the survival rate was miniscule. They kept looking at us as if we were rare birds, but they were gracious and hospitable.

Andrej ran home to get documents and albums that he had collected from survivors of the death march. He is an expert on the stories about the "Evacuation." He hosts a Facebook page and an annual memorial ceremony on the third Sunday in September.

Andrej mentioned his ancestors were named Santotsia or similar, and thought it was lovely that maybe we were related. He knows the geography and history of his prefecture and he told us the location of the prison, Wehjerowo, and indeed, we found it the next day. He also advised us about how to find the one and only hill in the flat beach town of Gdinya.

Marcin, the musician-blogger, learned that the last months of the war were chaotic, with a panicked retreat due to the proximity of the Russian army. The soldiers had enormous challenges dealing with the columns of prisoners. There were sometimes 10,000 people in one column, with only 40 soldiers for all the prisoners. It seems that these soldiers did not have proper supplies themselves during the march so they accepted food, vodka, etc. as barter for setting some prisoners free. Each commander seemed to make his own haphazard decisions during the march and they slept wherever they could find a space large enough for the thousands of prisoners. While it does not seem logical to burden a military retreat with hundreds of thousands of prisoners, I learned that the German command wanted to capitalize on the slave labor back in Germany.

Gdinya After liberation in Chynowie, in exchange for the promise of a ride back to Kovno, Mom and her friends agreed to work for the Russian soldiers in the city of Gdinya, on the Baltic Coast, near Gdansk. The Russians had them guard a warehouse which held war booty stolen and stored by the Germans. She described the building as a multi-floor structure, which was previously a school. She also mentioned that when delivering the booty by horse and carriage to the train station, for shipment to Russia, they went "downhill." Those were the only clues we had from Mom's narrative. So, we set out to find two main places: a train station "downhill" from an old school building.

The city of Gdinya is a Baltic sea resort at sea level—and it is totally flat. Our guide, Michal, found the one and only hill based on the mayor's instructions, and Google Maps. He took us to the train line and found one road which led uphill from the station. We were shocked to discover that there was not one, but, three schools on this road. No one had any information or knowledge about the history of the buildings during the Second World War. We could only guess which building might have been the correct one. We decided that the correct building was the one which had multiple floors, according to Mom's description. And indeed, the road from the school door led directly down to the main train station of Gdinya. We were fairly sure that we were on the correct street and had found that famous train station near where Zlata and Feival had their implausibly coincidental reunion.

Reflections on the Journey How did I feel being in Lithuania and Poland? I kept asking myself this question, and many others asked me the same. I must admit that it felt oddly familiar! My culinary senses were ignited by the food which reminded me of my mother's kitchen: herrings of all kinds, white pot cheeses, the delicious black Lithuanian bread, potato pancakes, *kreplach* (*pirogi* in Polish), both types of *borscht*, and *blintzes*.

I loved going into the bakery shops, which reminded me of Israel. I noticed the jelly donuts in the window, called *ponchkes*—the Polish word my mother-in-law used for the Hebrew *sufganiot*, which are the traditional fried jelly donuts served on Hanukah. I saw my mother-in-law's famous cheesecake, called *Sernik*. And on every street corner, the ubiquitous *bagele* vendors—just like in Tel Aviv. I realized just how strong this Eastern European influence is in Israel.

As I love history and shopping, wherever I travel I search for antique shops and enjoy browsing and buying my souvenirs. However, in Poland, I got the creeps every time I walked into an antique shop. Where did all this stuff come from? Who were the previous owners? Just like whenever I'm meeting young Germans, Lithuanians or Poles, I always wonder "what was your grandfather doing 75 years ago?" Was he in the SS stationed in Lithuania or Poland? How much blood does he have on his hands? But as I remind myself, the younger generation should not be held responsible for the deeds of their ancestors, right? I came to that realization many years ago. But then there is the Polish government and the new laws of 2018, declaring it a crime to say that the Poles had any responsibility in the genocide of the Jews. And in Lithuania many of the murderers themselves have achieved high-ranking positions or have their names on street signs today and, by contrast, some Jewish partisan fighters have been tagged for crimes against humanity. Really? This is difficult for me to accept.

I have made a number of presentations about my genealogical research, my planning and my travels in the footsteps of my family. After hearing the story, some 2Gs have mentioned that they, too, would want to undertake a similar project, but lamented the lack of funds, information, time, or courage. I do, indeed, realize how lucky I am to have received so much information from my parents and grandparents, allowing me to build upon that baseline. Most 2Gs do not have this starting point, so the research is much more complicated. And, of course, at this time, most of the survivors have already passed and can no longer give testimony.

However, I have always believed that if there is a will, there is a way. I encourage descendants who are interested in genealogy or travelling to countries of their ancestors to do as much research as they can beforehand. It was very helpful for me to subscribe to platforms such as JewishGen, Ancestry.com and a host of other databases. In addition, Facebook has numerous groups for the Second Generation or specifically for countries or towns of ancestry. You would be surprised what data is now available online or from other researchers.

Needless to say, it is imperative to interview all of the senior members of the family before it is too late. Even old neighbors or schoolmates can offer information about the family. Even if it is painful, they are usually very willing to tell their stories—if they are asked; they want their story to be told, especially in their older years. In addition, one must establish a plan with specific outcomes and make local contacts to assist in the research. As for funding, this is a personal challenge and sometimes a question of priorities and creativity. Some local guides organize regional group tours, which can cut the costs. But, indeed, to tailor the trip and travel on your own is not inexpensive. I encourage anyone who is interested to start researching now!

This trip was a monumental project for me. I can now visualize the stories, the locations and the history of my parents' lives before, during and after the war. This trip filled in the "holes" in my imagination and gave me an opportunity to know my parents better. And the writing and researching of this memoir have reinforced for me just what an incredible person my mother was. She survived unspeakable atrocities—but she was strong and incredibly resilient, always maintaining a healthy balance of reality, determination, optimism, humor and infinite, unconditional love for everyone in her family and close circle of friends.

My trip was exciting, fulfilling, emotional and educational. I found what I came to find ... but, let's just say, I will not return. Oh, Mama, I wish you were here to tell me your thoughts now; I hope you would approve.

---

1. Desbois, 2008
2. Chinov stories corroborated by Galperin, N. , 1989 and Drywa, D., p. 241

PART III

THE SECOND GENERATION (2G): THE IMPACT OF MY FAMILY'S HOLOCAUST EXPERIENCES ON ME

INTRODUCTION

At the time of writing, it has been 73 years since the end of World War II and most of the Jewish survivors have passed on and are, hopefully, at peace after their life struggles. Even the child-survivors, who might now be in their 70s or 80s, are infirm or elderly. Soon there will be no one left to bear witness. Thus, it is up to us, the Second Generation, and subsequently, the Third Generation, to ensure that their stories are told to descendants and to the whole world, and that the Holocaust cannot be denied, minimized, or forgotten. These are the main goals of this memoir.

Over the last 40 years, there has been growing interest in us—the Second Generation, and now even the Third Generation. Why this interest? Certainly, it could be because we are the ones who can continue to tell the stories about our families. But there is another reason for this interest. There is a growing body of research about the effects of this horrific period of time, not only on the survivors, but also on subsequent generations. The question is, is there an intergenerational transmission of trauma and resilience? Are traumatic experiences of the parents passed on to their offspring?

Originally, it was believed that the behavior of parents influences the behavior of offspring. That is, growing up and hearing about the war experiences of the parents and observing any post-traumatic behavior were seen as catalysts for specific common behaviors among the offspring. I certainly believed that, especially after reading *Children of the Holocaust* by Helen Epstein, and then a subsequent book by Aron Haas, *In the Shadow of the Holocaust*. I could identify with the numerous interviewees—all Second Generation, like myself. I learned about the commonalities of much of our parents' behaviors, idiosyncrasies, fears, moods, nightmares, outbursts, and integration into their new societies. Reading these books catapulted me into a familiar culture. Some of the experiences of the interviewees sounded much like my own. I felt like a member of this club of children whose major bond was the Jewish European history and trauma that our parents experienced. We were describing thoughts about an event to which we were not witnesses. However, I must say that after reading anecdotes about some extreme parental behaviors, I remember thinking, Wow, I am glad my parents weren't like that!

Today, with the advances in technology, there are greater possibilities to observe and measure changes in the body resulting from trauma. Since trauma can change body chemistry, how does it impact DNA? The study of epigenetics focuses on chemical changes at the cellular level. The hypothesis is that modified DNA might be passed on to the next generation and there is great interest in continuing research on this hypothesis.[1]

In a book about her grandparents' survival, Tammy Bottner described her inexplicable and irrational fear for the safety of her newborn child, as if she were a survivor herself—but she wasn't. She is Third Generation. Similarly, after my children were born, I had a terrible twinge of foreboding, which had no rational explanation. I feel the same tweak at my heart while watching my grandchildren growing up. Sometimes, I get a feeling as if I had lived through the dark days of my parents' trauma—with fleeting fears and thoughts. As some of us, particularly those born shortly after liberation, may say: "We feel as if we experienced the Holocaust." It is inexplicable, but since this response is repeated, even among complete strangers, it cannot be a coincidence. So, is it because of nurture or nature that we experience a feeling of foreboding or *déjà vu*?

I have no expertise in the science of the chemical effects of trauma, but perhaps we are learning that the age-old debate about nurture versus nature is now tipped in a different direction—toward the genetic-physiological intergenerational effects of trauma. I look forward to more research.

Indeed, I have the auspicious status of being one of the thousands of babies born after the war to Jewish survivors recuperating and reconnecting in some of the hundreds of Displaced Persons camps established throughout Germany, Austria and Italy in response to the enormous refugee crisis. Camps were set up from 1945, with most closing in 1950, with some remaining in operation even longer. Thousands of female survivors, with similar horrific and torturous experiences to my mother, worried that they would not be able to bear children. I was the precious child my mother never thought she would be able to have. And, as was very common among survivors, she named me after her mother who was murdered in Birkenau (Auschwitz) in 1944.

So I was their firstborn, born on European soil, during the time that my parents were recuperating and searching for a country which would accept them as immigrants. At first they thought to immigrate to Palestine/Israel. But when they finally received visas for the USA, my mother decided that she would rather not go to a country at war and with little food, especially with a baby in tow.

I was the one born closest to their trauma, liberation, and their physical rehabilitation. And for the last 35 years, I have fervently researched the family genealogy, family history and the impact of the Holocaust on the Second Generation. I have tried to analyze my parents' behavior, parenting and nurturing, storytelling, friends, lifestyle, migrations, relationship with Israel, fears and traumas, and its effects on my beliefs, behavior, emotions, career choices and parenting.

One of the major revelations from this exercise is that I learned just how difficult it is to separate the impact of their Holocaust experiences from the immigrant-refugee experiences in their new country. My reflections and analysis follow herein.

---

1. For more about epigenetics, see Rodriguez, T; Kellerman, N.P.; Baack, G.A.

CONNECTION TO FAMILY, HISTORY AND HERITAGE

As soon as I became of school age, Mom enrolled me in *Yiddishe Shule* (Yiddish school). It was extremely important to her that I become literate in the literature and language of our family and familiar with the culture of Jewish life in Eastern Europe. I attended this supplemental schooling for seven years, travelling alone on buses and subways, in Brooklyn and Manhattan, from an early age. Mama was so proud of her daughter's language skills and whenever they were visiting, she would have me speak Yiddish to her friends. She was thrilled when I wrote letters in Yiddish to my grandparents in Israel or spoke to them in Yiddish over my father's "ham" amateur radio, and when I performed in the "Third Seder" on stage at the Waldorf Astoria on Passover—and all in Yiddish.

Mom was fastidious about keeping all Jewish holiday traditions and always made big dinners for friends and relatives. She served all the traditional foods for which she became well known, including the ubiquitous chicken soup with either *matza* balls, *lokshen* (noodles) or *kreplach* (meat-ravioli), *tsimmes* (cooked, sweet carrots), *kugels* (quiches) of all kinds, herrings, *cholent*, and her pride and joy, *gefilte* fish. The one recipe that she was uniquely famous for, especially among her Lithuanian friends, was the

Lithuanian favorite sweet *teiglach* (little knots of dough cooked in honey with spices). She was so proud when everyone licked their fingers and commented on her skill of maintaining this lost cultural and gastronomical artifact.

As did many survivors, Mom named me after her mother, Eta, and my younger sister, Jeanne, after her father, Yankel, or Yakov, who were murdered in the war. The family joke was that she wanted to name my sister Jacqueline, but could not spell it at the time. By the time my youngest sister was born in 1962, Mama accepted my suggestion for the name, Rena—simply because we liked it and without any historical or family connection.

Maintaining contact with Mom's only surviving relative, her sister, and also her in-laws in Israel was an extremely important part of our lives. We recognized that we were one of the very few survivor families which actually had a set of grandparents and siblings who also survived. Letters were constantly coming and going on those onion-thin blue aerogramme papers. Eventually, my grandparents came to live with us for a short time, and then my aunt and her family immigrated to the USA. Few could afford to travel in those early years, so funds were always saved and earmarked for a future trip to Israel—I was the first family visitor to Israel in 1965. And in 1970 my parents and sisters made *Aliya* (immigrated) to Israel and reunited with my father's family. I joined them the following year.

Mom's relationship with her only surviving family member was the tightest of bonds. While they did not agree on many things, she and her sister, Nechama, adored each other and would let nothing stand in the way of their love. When Mom realized that her sister was not well, she insisted on going to visit her, despite the distance, the cost of a flight from Israel to New York, and despite the fact that she herself was losing brain power. It was as if she knew that this would be their last meeting.

We had many relatives all over the world: in the USA, Israel, Argentina, Uruguay, South Africa and in Lithuania (USSR). They were fortunate to have left Lithuania, or Belarus, many years before the war. Mom kept in contact with them all, even her only surviving uncle in her hometown of Kaunas, Lithuania. She feared sending letters directly to the USSR from the USA, so they would communicate via relatives in Israel. She continuously asked relatives, who had not been affected by the war, to send her copies of any pre-war photos that they had received from her family. These photos became holy family artifacts and hung in individually collected antique frames on the walls in all the homes in which we lived; she had quite a large wall collection, and she had quite a number of relocations.

My mother had an impressive memory for details about each member of the family. She conscientiously listed and recorded all the names of those who were murdered in the Holocaust. She submitted "Pages of Testimony" to Yad Vashem, to the U.S. Holocaust Memorial Museum and family names for a monument in Miami. She submitted photos and documentation to various other Holocaust museums as well. Once a fellow worker gave her an envelope with photos of atrocities from the Ohrdruf concentration camp in Germany. As a soldier in the U.S. Army, he took these photos when he liberated the camp. Now that he was aging, he wanted her to "do something" with them. She donated them in his name to the U.S. Holocaust Memorial Museum.

My mother, father and youngest sister attended the American Gathering of Jewish Holocaust Survivors in 1983, in Washington, D.C. She never missed a memorial event for Lithuanian Jews on the special commemoration dates, either in New York or in Tel Aviv. She served on the committee for the Israeli Association of Lithuanian Jews. In 1995, they organized a huge event to commemorate 50 years of liberation. She also spoke to adult and youth audiences about her experiences. She felt it was her duty—her obligation—as a survivor to remember and name those who did not survive and also, tell the world the details of a history which should not be forgotten.

Many survivors did not want to tell their stories to their children, perhaps to spare them the burden of the horror; others did not tell the stories, perhaps to spare themselves more pain. However, Mama felt strongly that each survivor should tell their children, regardless of their personal pain, and was very upset when she learned about those who did not—even among her close friends. Mom encouraged us to read about and watch movies or documentaries about the Holocaust. However, when watching Hollywood accounts, like the TV series "Holocaust," I distinctly remember her saying: "That's a concentration camp? It looks like a summer camp, not a concentration camp."

Throughout my life, I heard fractured pieces of the story from my parents, and through their conversations with friends. And then, for the first time, in 2004, we convinced her to be interviewed and recorded in order to document her complete story for her descendants. She agreed; this was the first time we heard the story from start to finish, in chronological order.

Impact As a dutiful child, I attended *Yiddishe Shule*. We learned to read and write in Yiddish and we read the Yiddish classics by Sholem Aleichem, Peretz, Menachem Mendel Sforim and others. We put on plays and learned all the traditional and war songs in Yiddish. Whenever I hear *Rozhinkes Mit Mandlen* (*Raisins and Almonds*) and, especially, *Zog Nit Kein Mol* (*The Partisan's Song*), I experience a visceral and emotional reaction—and I often find myself sobbing uncontrollably. My connection to this culture is deep in my soul.

I did not complain about going to *Yiddishe Shule*, even though I resented not being elsewhere with school friends. I knew it was important to Mama and I recall being proud of my skills and being glad that I could make her so very happy and proud at these moments. I always tried to make Mama happy. But, truth be told, I sometimes felt more comfortable among the children of survivors and immigrants, than with my American friends. Even from those early years, I recall feeling the need to hide the fact that I was Jewish from the non-Jewish world. I felt good about being a chameleon—i.e. not "looking" Jewish to the outside world, or being able to "pass" for a non-Jew. I felt safer this way.

Loyalty and responsibility to family was an imperative in the family. We could never say "no" to family. Mom said: "Your mother is your best friend; I wish I had my mother now." There was not much I could say in response.

My connection to Israel continued throughout my life. In my Brooklyn elementary school, P.S. 235, we participated in a school-sponsored savings program whereby we brought in $1 each week and watched the numbers accumulated in our individual bank books. From early on, my mother told me that this account was earmarked for my future trip to Israel. And indeed, when I was 16, I visited my grandparents, aunt, uncle and cousins. I so enjoyed this wonderful experience that I did not want to return at the end of the summer break. I was so proud to have been the first of any of my friends to fly overseas and I wanted to tell them stories about life in Israel and international travel—but most were not really interested.

I recall waking up on the morning of the start of the Six-Day War in 1967 and being deeply worried, especially when my father said he wanted to go and help. I was even more disturbed when I learned that no one else in my American world even cared. This love for Israel was so deep, that when my parents decided to immigrate to Israel with my sisters, in 1970, I immediately agreed to join them. I eventually married and had three children in Israel. Despite our departure from Israel many years ago, this deeply rooted love of Israel, Hebrew and our culture has been transferred to all three of my children.

As a result of my mother's fervor in maintaining Lithuanian Jewish culture in our family, I learned to make many of the traditional recipes and maintained family holidays and customs. After living in Israel, my recipes include Israeli fare. We were never religious followers in Israel, never attended synagogue, and rarely celebrated a formal Shabbat, but we always celebrated the holidays, as did all other secular Israelis. However, when we relocated from Israel to

Singapore, I insisted that we celebrate Shabbat eve and attend synagogue for the holidays. I believed that this was one way we could preserve something of our Jewish-Israeli culture in our children among the innumerable cultures of their international school classmates. My children were born in Israel, raised internationally, became multilingual, and feel attached to Israel; in fact, one son focuses his writing career on the Middle East, and two of my children are raising their children to be multilingual. I am very proud of them.

On my grandfather's deathbed in Israel, I decided that it was imperative to get information about his ancestry. Thus, I interviewed him and he drew a pencil rendering of his family tree, which included his eleven siblings, parents, grandparents, cousins, uncles and aunts. My mother's memory of family names also helped me research her lineage. These served as the basis of my *entrée* into our family's genealogy in 1978, which I have continued passionately until today. At present, I have almost 880 names on the tree, and continue to search for and find more relatives worldwide. This has also become a family joke: "So what new relative have you found this week, Ettie?"

All the family photos have now been scanned, labelled and uploaded to folders and also to a genealogy platform, each aligned with the details I have researched on each person who is a blood relation. I hope that my descendants will cherish and maintain it, with the same respect, if not the same fervor.

I adored my grandfather, so, after he died in 1979, I wanted to continue the Jewish tradition and name my son after him. Clearly, I would not name my son Feival, so I researched the origin of the name. Feival means "bright one" in Hebrew, and also from the Greek, Feibus, who was the God of the sun. Thus, we named our son Neri, which means "my candle," or, "my light," in Hebrew. Fortuitously, he was born on Hanukah—the festival of lights.

As a student, I wrote essays about the Holocaust and my family's experience. As an adult, I immigrated to Israel, married an Israeli and had three children there. I eventually was accepted for a position at the Museum of the Jewish Diaspora, where I guided visitors through the various stations of Jewish history and conducted workshops on Jewish identity. I became fascinated by so much of Jewish history which I had never learned. So, I continued to read and research the Holocaust and Jewish history, simply to educate myself and better understand the 2000+ years of history and migrations. To this day, I give presentations about the Holocaust at conferences and schools, and participate in 2G discussion groups, Yom Hashoa (Holocaust Day) and Litvak memorial events.

I felt the imperative and the responsibility to interview, research, document, analyze, educate and tell the stories that I was told by my parents, my surviving relatives, and so many others who shared their testimonies and their research. I feel very fortunate to have received first-hand information to help me in my research and satisfy my curiosity. Unfortunately, I have learned that many 2Gs are not necessarily knowledgeable about the details of their history. Certainly, there are good reasons, as many were never given any details of their parents' war experiences, or the information was very sketchy. It is a pity, but in most cases, it is too late to get first-hand testimonies.

In order to ensure that we got the full story directly from Mama, my sister, Jeanne, interviewed and recorded her and I wrote the manuscript. And as I have also documented in this book, I embarked on my first trip to Lithuania and Poland "in my mother's footsteps." I travelled to Kovno, the remains of the Kovno ghetto, and Vilna in Lithuania. I also visited Stutthof concentration camp, the towns along the death march, Auschwitz-Birkenau concentration camps, and Gdinya, in Poland. On a prior trip, I visited the Dachau concentration camp, which is near the town where I was born in the Landsberg am Lech DP camp.

Perhaps because of the location of my birth in a DP camp—before our immigration to the U.S.; perhaps because of my birth order and the proximity of my birth to the horror, just four years after liberation and three years after full freedom; perhaps because I carried the name of my mother's mother, Eta, who was murdered in Auschwitz-Birkenau; or perhaps because of my academic training —I took on the dual roles of family chronicler, to record the Holocaust, and family genealogist, to find the forgotten members of my parents' lineage. I recall feeling that as my grandmother's namesake, I had a special responsibility—obligation—to maintain the family legacy. As an educator, I encourage my students and their families to do the same—regardless of their ethnic origin.

IMMIGRATION, LANGUAGES AND INTEGRATION

I grew up with the knowledge that my parents (and grandparents) were all multilingual. They were each literate in Yiddish, Lithuanian, Russian, German and Polish. My father learned English in school and through his amateur radio hobby, right after the war. Everyone learned Hebrew after immigrating to Israel. Through their stories I learned that their language skills helped them get work, possibly saving their lives, and helped them integrate into different societies. Thus, the importance of knowing languages was impressed upon me and I fostered this skill.

I always noticed, even as a child, that my thoughts and emotions were different from those of my American friends; my family was different. Why? We were obviously different from our American non-Jewish neighbors, employers, and colleagues, who understood that we were immigrants, with some making efforts to support our integration into American society. We were clearly different from other Jewish Americans who had no direct Holocaust experience and had been born in the U.S. or had immigrated at a young age before the Second World War. And while some of my parents' best friends were also immigrants and survivors from the "old country" they were somewhat different from them as well. Why? Firstly, my parents had relationships and developed strong friendships with Americans—both Jewish and non-Jewish. Secondly, my parents were two of the few immigrants who actually learned to speak grammatically correct English—and without an accent. This was probably a manifestation of their ear for languages and desire to integrate into American society.

During the citizenship process, my mother made sure to Americanize our European-sounding names to ease our integration and acceptance. Thus, Zlata became Lottie, Liova became Louis, and I, Eta, unfortunately, had to live with the legal name, Ethel.

Impact I was in awe of my parents' and grandparents' language skills and how it played a role in their survival and economics. It was while I was studying Spanish in junior high school that I developed my first "precocious" hypothesis of language acquisition: i.e. anyone who grows up with two languages can learn additional languages easily. I watched my monolingual classmates struggle with Spanish, while I found it fun and easy to learn. I subsequently studied French in high school and at university, learned Hebrew after immigrating to Israel, and had no trouble converting my Yiddish to German during visits to Germany and Austria. I learned survival Japanese before a trip to Japan, enjoyed playing with Bahasa vocabulary while living in Singapore, and learned to speak Chinese fairly fluently during my four years in Beijing. I eventually earned an additional university degree in second language acquisition and I worked in international schools with language immersion programs in six countries. For me, knowing languages allowed me to integrate into each foreign culture. And in the U.S., I could speak like a real Yankee, and no one would know I was Jewish. I wondered if these were my own survival strategies. Not surprisingly, I also ensured that my children were multilingual.

In elementary school, I was immediately tagged and pulled out for "speech" classes, because they claimed that I spoke with a "Jewish accent." Today, most enlightened schools would keep their English as a Second Language student mainstreamed in the classroom. To add insult to injury, at some time in the '50s, I was strongly affected by a school administrator, in P.S. 235 in Brooklyn, who made it a point to come into my classroom at the beginning of each year, and publicly ask the class: "Who was not born in the U.S.?" I was always the only one who raised her hand and had to respond that I was born in Germany. Needless to say, at that age and at that time, the kids started to call me "Nazi." After a long career in education, this memory left an indelible impression, and consequently ensured that no student would ever be embarrassed in public—for any reason.

From a young age, I began to understand that I was part of a minority in the U.S. I learned the skills of adaptation and felt like a chameleon, switching, adapting and fitting into both communities, languages and cultures. Thus, I understand and empathize with others who struggle because they are different. That includes immigrants, the disabled, second language learners, expatriates, and minorities.

It came as no surprise that I absolutely loved working in international schools in six countries. My friends, colleagues, the students and the parents were all, in one way or another, struggling with a new language, being different, adapting to life in a different culture and country, and being part of a minority culture within the majority environment. I embraced this diversity and I understood their challenges. I also understood and empathized with the students in my schools, who relocated with their parents as a result of their parents' careers and occupations. The monikers for these children, in research over the last 50 years, are Third Culture Kids, Cross-Cultural Kids or Global Nomads. I enjoyed helping the staff and students (and their parents) understand the challenges and benefits of their differences. Thus, I devoted my doctoral research and a subsequent book to these unique people.[1]

I also realized that I have a strong affinity towards anyone who has experienced family historical trauma, like American Indians, and Cambodian and Vietnamese refugees. I am able to understand, empathize and bond with those who have had the immigrant-refugee-survivor experience. While each story is different, the residual effects have many similarities.

Continuing with my fascination on cross-cultural themes, I conducted another research project where I identified the catalysts for choosing an international career. The primary catalyst is what I termed, "Wonder With the Wide World (W4)."[2] I believe that my own W4 and *wanderlust* stem from my parents' stories of living in, escaping from and immigrating to different countries, language fluency, having relatives in six countries and my father's passion for speaking to the world on his "ham" radio.

---

1. See Zilber, www.ettiezilber.com/books.
2. See Zilber, https://www.ettiezilber.com/publication-1/

PHYSICAL AND MENTAL HEALTH

My mother told me that after the war, she never thought she would be able to have a child, due to the years of slave labor, physical abuse, stress, fear, frostbite, typhus, lice infestation, scabies, and malnutrition—actually starvation—and amenorrhea. I remember once, during my teen years, asking my mother how she cared for herself when she menstruated during the war. In a casual way, she told me that she was "lucky" that her period stopped during the war. She later understood that it was because of her extreme weight loss, combined with the low body fat and stress, which caused amenorrhea. Today, we are familiar with this symptom in girls with anorexia.

And then, there were Papa's angry outbursts. Often they appeared without an obvious cause, sometimes with a specific trigger. Today, we understand these behaviors as PTSD. I vividly remember Mom's nighttime dreaming, screaming and awakening in terror; it lessened, but would never completely stop throughout her life. But she did not believe in psychiatrists; she believed in work therapy. So, if she was upset, nostalgic, sad, grieving or agitated, she would clean, iron, scrub the floors, cook or find some other work in the home or the garden. She never sat idle or rested—ever!

And Mom was compulsive about fixing and caring for her teeth. She was embarrassed by her ugly teeth even before the war, but, during the war, her teeth suffered from her malnutrition and lack of hygiene. Before she fixed her teeth she never smiled in photos and often covered her mouth when she spoke. Both for reasons of vanity and health, one of the first things she did after immigration, and after some savings, was to begin the painful and expensive process of fixing her teeth and gums. This same preoccupation extended to her children, introducing us all to dentists from a young age.

Mom always laughed when she told us about her check-up visits to doctors. The doctors would ask her if anyone in her family had cancer, or any other diseases. She would smile and gently have to tell them that they had no time to develop a disease; they were killed young.

Impact I always took care to eat a healthy diet, and I became meticulous with my own children in preparing only healthy food options for them. I was trained as a teacher of Health and Physical Education, thus, I was aware of proper nutrition and never allowed sodas, candies and other snacks into our home. I became a good cook and homemaker as well, but I could never hold a candle to my mother. And I, too, was fastidious about taking care of my own and my children's teeth from an early age. Gratefully, they each have healthy teeth today and I continue to support the lifestyles of my numerous dentists.

I recall my nightmares about an undefined war, or dangerous situation, where my family was in mortal danger. In the dream, I believed that I was some kind of super-hero, who could save them. Or I would dream about my own survival; could I survive what my parents did? I no longer have these dreams, but I do occasionally have fleeting thoughts of potential disaster and plan what I would do if ...

And Mom's stories about her continual fight against lice and typhus were not lost on me. As a parent and educational leader, I became an expert at identifying and fighting the head lice epidemics that plagued our homes and schools. I did not recoil in horror when faced with a scalp full of nits or lice, as would other adults, rather I would address the issue before and after the fact. Perhaps it was a small war that I was fighting on my own terms. But I remember how mortified my mother was when she visited and learned that my children brought lice home from school. Of course, they were not body lice, but it shocked her all the same!

And I, too, am a great believer in work and keeping busy, both for mental balance and getting things done. I always recall my mother's belief in work therapy and idleness avoidance, so, consequently, I have been very productive.

RISK TAKING, PLUCK AND RESILIENCE

Needless to say, every single survivor has many stories of adversity, challenges, luck and serendipity. All had stories of how they avoided arrest, capture, punishment, starvation, death, or how they took risks. Some simply declared that they did what they had to do to survive—everything, during those years, was life-threatening. My mother believed that "you had to adapt or you would be lost." This was another one of her mantras.

My mother told us numerous stories about risk-taking at various times during our childhood and through her recorded testimony, such as her mother's need for an abortion in the ghetto—without any anesthesia—and without making a sound; bringing arms into the ghetto; hiding her wedding ring in the concentration camp; hiding their money in the latrine; hiding unsuccessfully in an underground *malina* (hideout) but coming out when they realized they would suffocate or burn to death, only to be captured by the Nazis and sent to the concentration camp; strategies to avoid certain rape, using a knife to threaten the *macher*, who took their money and did not deliver the needed documents, their friends' escape from the Ninth Fort killing field to the ghetto, Papa's escape from the ghetto, Papa eating raw eggs to survive, Papa walking up to an SS soldier guarding the bridge, asking him for a light and then casually sauntering across to the city, Mom's illegal border crossing from the American to the Soviet zone to find my father, jumping on a military train that was already moving, and more. All these stories were stories of risk, pluck and resilience, and they were told to us, as if there was a message; most likely there was—you do what you have to do to survive and you never give up.

Mom had a number of mottos. I always repeated the mantra I attributed to my mother: "Whatever doesn't kill you makes you strong." Imagine my surprise when I learned that Nietzsche took the words right out of her mouth; but I continue to recite Mom's mantra to all who will listen. Another motto was: "If they ask you if you can do something, say yes. You can always learn how afterwards." And then, there was her continuous philosophy of life: "Keep working, keep moving and keep walking." She kept this mantra through her last years. Even in her dementia fog at 90 years old, she seemed to know that walking was an imperative.

Mama's challenges did not end in New York harbor, gazing at the Statue of Liberty; in fact, like most immigrants without money or language, her challenges began anew at that moment. But she persevered and faced each day by adapting and putting one foot in front of the other.

Impact Demonstrating *chutzpa* (pluck) was highly regarded and praised in my family. I have been raised to be strong, independent, fearless and resilient. While I had many fears, I learned to overcome them and do whatever I have to do, whether it is packing up the house, relocating and living in multiple foreign countries, nurturing tiny premature twins, dealing with the real threat of terrorism, getting through wars in Israel, adjusting after a house fire, killing mice, scorpions, snakes and cockroaches and dealing with lice, worms and other afflictions. And, in my professional careers, the mantra was the same. I am proud of the fact that no matter how challenging the situation, I deal with it; I believe that I can get through it; and, I never give up. I have also learned to fail and get back up on my feet and try again, and adapt to almost any situation. I attribute all this to my mother's example.

Watching my parents as they navigated their way as immigrants through the new culture and language of the U.S., and then at a later age to Israel, clearly had an impact on me. I was a front row observer of their difficulties, challenges and resilience and subsequently, I, myself, relocated and migrated in and out of six countries and travelled to 65. I have developed an insatiable need to travel, to experience the excitement of different cultures and test myself in each. That includes learning languages and finding my way around the country. And, as my mother taught me, I always adapted to every situation and location.

Due to my parents' war stories, I actually started testing myself from a young age. I recall one specific day in high school. I know it was a Monday because I was carrying my clean physical education uniform, sneakers and socks in my school bag. There had just been heavy snowfall and the temperature was sub-zero. I was walking the mile to my school and I was wearing a skirt, as girls were not allowed to wear pants in those years. My toes were frozen in my boots and I could have stopped to put on the extra pair of socks. However, I refused, as I wanted to see if I could survive the walk to school and frozen toes, like my mother survived the freezing cold death march. Strange, right? When I told my mother about it, she was shocked beyond words.

While living in Israel, I became trained in rifle shooting and range supervision; my husband and I later had guns in the home to protect ourselves from the real possibility of a terrorist attack. I played scenarios in my head about what I should do, just in case. I would often see danger around the corner, such as driving under a bridge on a highway, imagining that it would collapse. So, I would think of an escape plan, just in case. Perhaps this is why I became adept at writing emergency preparedness manuals and practicing drills at the schools I led.

Baack (2016) combined 37 traits of a resilient person with the concepts of social construction and post-traumatic growth, and developed a new definition of resilience based on "a process of surviving and moving forward from trauma that is far different than 'bouncing back." (p. 146) From Baack's list and the new definition of a resilient person, I recognized my mother, myself and my children in most of them.

PERSPECTIVE ON HUMAN NATURE AND GOVERNMENT

Needless to say, experiencing how life could be turned upside down within an instant—after the collapse of their country, their government, their democratic laws, their military, after being conquered by an enemy force, friends and family members disappearing, tortured and/or murdered—made my parents cynical about life, human nature and distrustful of any form of government or leadership. There was always a sense that life was tenuous and insecure, and that we should not expect much from the world, people or the government. We could only trust ourselves. My mother repeated her father's warning to me: "Never join any political organization." And another one of her famous Yiddish proverbs was *a mentsch tracht undt Gott lacht*, which translates literally as "A person plans and God laughs." However, the message had a deeper meaning, that despite one's planning and preparation, life could deal you a blow at any time. Interestingly, she harbored a deep distrust and cynicism, yet she was basically an optimistic person.

My parents also emphasized that the first attacks and murders against the Jews in Lithuania were perpetrated on the streets of Kovno by Lithuanians, even before the Germans arrived. Many were neighbors—even high school classmates. In fact, my mother described identifying one of her classmates guarding the prisoners with a rifle after she and her family were imprisoned in the Seventh Fort; she was a witness to the massacres as well. Neighbors took over Jewish homes and possessions just as the massacres were taking place and after the Jews were relocated and imprisoned in the ghetto a few months later. And, of course, there was her huge disappointment when one of her own friends stole her father's watch from her home after the war.

Mom told stories about the various times she had to cross borders illegally in order to find Papa, or get to safety and freedom, or when she had to deal with the authorities during or after the war. Of course, her actions were fraught with fear and danger, but she did what she had to. I recall, in our early years in the USA, her fear and uncertainty whenever she had to deal with bureaucrats and authorities. It was an automatic response, which she had to overcome—and she did.

When my parents finally reunited in Kovno after the war, their first impulse was to return to their homes. However, many houses were already occupied by neighbors or other townspeople and the contents were stolen—or "relocated". My parents heard stories about survivors who were killed after the war when they returned to reclaim their properties. So my parents decided that it was not worth getting killed for property—especially after their ordeal. They emphasized this by repeating the story numerous times.

My mother continued to hate anything German and boycotted all German products. It wasn't until we moved to Israel that she accepted my purchase of a Volkswagen, rationalizing that if Israel was accepting money, buses and machinery from Germany, then she would accept this purchase. Nevertheless, she would still become upset when any one of us travelled to or through Germany, or with the German airline. She would never, ever consider visiting Lithuania, as did some of her friends who vacationed there in their later years.

And then there were stories of those who secretly helped by giving refuge, food or other acts of kindness, despite the dangers. Other than from her camp-mates and the Russian couple which occupied her home, Mom did not recount any acts of kindness or support, but my father did, after his escape from the ghetto.

Impact I recall many of my friends joining political organizations in the '60s and '70s protesting the war in Vietnam. Some were very politically active. However, always mindful of my parents' admonitions, I never became active, never joined any political party, nor signed any petition—until recently, at 69 years of age.

My parents always reiterated that "it could happen here." When I was younger, I could not imagine this eventuality. At school, I was educated to believe that America was the best country in the world; we were a democracy, and such atrocities and behaviors could never happen here; we were always the good guys—I was safe here. However, as I get older, I have become extremely sensitive to changes in the political climate. If any country elects an autocratic leader, I get anxious. In my gut, I maintain a deep-seated fear that there may be dangers around the corner—even in a democratic society. After all, Hitler came to power through democratic elections.

My stomach churned when I read about the Neo-Nazis marching in the town of Skokie, Illinois, in 1977, and still does when I see the huge uptick in anti-Semitic acts of vandalism and murder. The recent spate of verbal and physical attacks on immigrants, Latinos, Muslims, blacks and Jews, switch my mind to somewhere I have been before. And the recent demonstrations by supremacist-hate groups in Charlottesville and elsewhere have caused me great anxiety. At times like these, I envision my parents' experiences and start thinking of exit strategies over and over in my head; that's when I realize just how much I have been affected by events that I never witnessed.

When I visited Kovno, as described in the previous chapter, I found the house which I believed to be that of my mother's family. In the backyard of the house was another house, as per my mother's testimony. A man saw us talking and pointing to the house; he came out of the house. I was stricken with an irrational fear of this man, so I did not ask him any of the usual questions about the history of the war or the house. I can only explain that my strange fear was the direct result of hearing the stories my parents told us of abuses and murders after the war. And despite the fact that I grew up in the U.S., I still get a strange feeling in the pit of my stomach whenever I have to pass through immigration or deal with authorities. That feeling lasts only a nanosecond; I have learned to put it out of my head—but it is my default emotion.

While I learned about the sadistic brutality of human behavior, I also recall being impressed by the struggle of some "Righteous Gentiles" to do good during a time of evil. In fact, I wrote an essay for my English class in high school about those who helped Jews during the Holocaust. I was surprised when my teacher complimented me on the essay, as he seemed extremely touched by it. I think I needed to believe that there were some acts of kindness, sacrifice and goodness, i.e. some ray of light during this time of darkness.

When I was younger, I categorically blamed those who did not help the Jews in their time of need. However, as I grew older, and had a family, I was, and still am, continuously plagued with the question of whether I would have risked my life or the lives of my family members to help someone in such a topsy-turvy political climate, where right was morally wrong and wrong was abhorrently right. I do not yet have an answer, but the older I get, the more I hesitate to give a dogmatic response.

FAMILY IDIOSYNCRASIES

Every family has its own cultural and behavioral idiosyncrasies. Ours might have been slightly different because of the Holocaust, or, as I mentioned before, because we were immigrants. As the oldest child, I was raised according to strict European-style parenting customs, e.g. strict curfews, no stockings, no lipstick, no short skirts, no nail polish, and other prohibitions. My sisters and I always joke about how our youngest sister (13 years my junior) was raised by "different" parents. By the time she became a teenager, my parents had been living the American dream for 25 years. Thus, she did not have the same prohibitions and does not have the same perspective at all.

My mother kept the house as sterile as an operating room, with everything in place, scrubbed, and with the contents of her closets in perfect military alignment. From her stories about trying to maintain some semblance of hygiene in the concentration camp, fear of lice and disease, and sacrificing her ersatz-coffee rations to wash her body, it was no wonder from whence came my mother's mania for cleanliness and keeping a spotless and organized home. Or perhaps this was symptomatic of her work mania and trauma.

My parents were also perfectionists. My mother demanded perfection in everything from me. While practicing piano, I remember her shouting from the kitchen "wrong!" every time I hit a wrong note. Every time I cut a loaf of bread, I am reminded of Mom's story about the precision with which she had to cut a loaf of bread and divide it perfectly among nine starving women in the concentration camp. And I recall her lessons on ironing, knitting, sewing, darning and cooking; everything had to be done perfectly—just like she learned during the war.

My father once scolded me for the imperfect way I washed my car. My ears still ring with his words: "That's how you wash a car? I will show you how to wash a car, the way the Germans taught me." And he proceeded to open the hood, inspect and make me polish the engine so it shined like a mirror. It was a strong statement from him, but not a punishable offense. It seemed more like a life lesson he wanted to impart to me—perhaps for my future survival—or just one of his sudden outbursts.

My father was a perfectionist with his work and his hobbies. He was totally immersed in his amateur radio. After work and after dinner, he would sit through the night speaking to people around the world. He was a fanatic about building his equipment himself, with the strongest signals and tallest antenna towers. He later transferred this passion and immersion to golf. While I cannot declare that this was a result of his war experiences, it certainly gave him a forum to separate himself from his past world and focus on the present one. And everything he did, he did to perfection.

My parents were also perfectionists regarding time. Clearly, my parents had to be punctual both for the ghetto work or roundup schedule, as well as in the concentration camp—under penalty of beatings or death. They continued to stick to this punctuality throughout their lives.

My mother did not have any jewelry in the early years in the U.S., nor many clothes, but she always had shoes. She loved shoes. Perhaps it was due to the war years when she had no proper footwear, even on the death march in the middle of the Polish winter. However, she would never, ever buy black leather boots or coats, or any blouse with stripes—and would not allow her daughters to wear them either. She also loved crystal and sought out lovely pieces at flea markets, perhaps to reconnect to the pieces in her parents' home. At the dentist's office, she refused nitrous oxide, commonly known as laughing gas, which was administered with a mask over the nose and mouth. The reasons seem obvious.

Perhaps a war remnant, or not, is the fact that my parents never closed the doors of any room in the house. If I closed the door to my bedroom, my mother would admonish me. I did not think it was strange until I read about a similar behavior in interviews with other 2Gs. As an older teenager, I started closing doors for my own privacy; at that point, my parents did not object.

My parents taught us about their own secret whistle, which they used in the ghetto in order to identify themselves or to warn of danger. In fact, during my parents' forbidden wedding in the ghetto, Papa's friends stood guard around the Santocki home and were prepared to use the whistle if any guards or soldiers came too close to the house. I used it throughout my childhood to communicate with family members, knowing full well its origin.[1]

Of course, food and cooking became a focal point for my mother. Indeed, she became an outstanding cook and baker and was very proud of her skill. Our fridge was always full of wonderful food, both from traditional and new American recipes. If I ever misspoke and said that I was hungry, I was told: "You don't know what it is to be hungry." After the years of starvation, she would eat large quantities and both she and my father would eat very fast and finish everything on their plates. If there was anything left over, my parents would finish it completely. And good dark bread was a staple they could not live without. Mom's greatest pleasure was tearing off a big piece of bread and eating it with lots of butter and jam—never, ever margarine.

Impact I always emulated my parents, as I was in awe of their resilience and strength after learning of the horrors of their lives.

However, the flip side was that I could never ask them for help with my mundane problems, which could never be compared to the problems and suffering they had endured. I also never wanted to burden them with my disappointments or difficulties—or anything negative; after all, they had it worse, and my petty problems paled by comparison. I don't remember if they ever articulated this attitude, but I certainly absorbed it, as did so many of the Second Generation that I read about. I also felt that since they had suffered so much, I had to shield them from further suffering, so I never wanted to tell them any bad news and always brought home excellent report cards. I always wanted to make them happy, almost as if to make up for their suffering. Teenage rebellion did not exist—at least not overtly.

I recall being envious of my American friends, who had so many aunts, uncles, cousins and grandparents. I was also jealous of those who had a dark basement or attic filled with old family relics. Perhaps that is why I became such an avid genealogist, and antique and art collector.

I, too, have a shoe fetish and will also not wear black leather jackets, coats or boots. I actually only bought my first pair of black boots at the age of 60 and recall having an internal battle as a result. I cannot bring myself to buy or wear anything with stripes either.

Everyone in my family eats quickly. Invariably, when we are dining in a social group, we are the first to finish everything on our plates. The family joke is that we "inhale" our food for fear of a *pogrom* (attack) by Cossacks at any minute. This behavior has been passed down to my children as well. We are a restaurant owner's dream. We eat fast and leave quickly. And I love bread.

Indeed, I am a perfectionist in many aspects of my life, homemaking and profession, but it is clear to me that I cannot even come close to the punctiliousness of my parents. My sisters and I joke about our family's definition of punctuality. It does not mean being on time, oh no! Punctuality means arriving at least fifteen minutes before the scheduled time. This punctuality is deeply embedded in each of us, to this day. Gratefully, with age, many of these idiosyncrasies have abated.

And I taught my children our family whistle, which is familiar and was used for many years for communication—until texting came along.

---

1. Mama taught us the ghetto whistle: do re mi fa so la; *zol leben di libe, hoora, hoora* (do re mi fa so la; love should prevail, hooray, hooray). This has remained our family whistle to this day.

ATTITUDE, HAPPINESS AND PRIORITIES

To my parents, their definition of happiness was when the family was physically together in the home. In fact, they would stay home a lot; that was their definition of "fun." In their stories, this was the most important factor in the war—being together. Mom told stories of how they had (illegal) gatherings at her home in the ghetto, with very little food, some vodka and a record player.

I remember that, whenever we were all together, there was a higher level of happiness in my parents' demeanor. We always joked and laughed as we sat around the dinner table. As children, my sister and I would perform songs for our parents, as we all made merry. My parents always found a reason to celebrate; Mom always said that as long as you have some vodka, potatoes, fat, onions, bones, and beans—you have a party. Since they could not afford a babysitter, they typically invited their friends to convene at their home. There was always music—always! In fact, my father's electronic skills with radios and TVs ensured that my parents always owned a reconstructed and recycled TV, radio or record player for entertainment.

Mom's view of life was of the cup half full; she also subscribed to the adage: "If life hands you lemons, make lemonade." And she always stressed: "Don't look back; move forward."

Another priority was that life, family and well-being were more important than property or collecting things. They never had a problem leaving their house and relocating elsewhere. I recall my father saying: "It is only a house."

My parents valued family above all else; they would do anything for family and close friends. Mom always kept up correspondence with her extended family, throughout the world. It was a happy day when a blue or gray aerogramme appeared in our mailbox and we would sit around the table as she read bits to us.

Each year on their anniversary on June 4, we heard my parents' love and marriage story. They met, fell in love and in a very short time, decided to have a traditional marriage. Under ordinary circumstances, this is not an unusual story, however, it took place in the ghetto, with a death penalty for marriages and where they did not know if they would live to see the next day. The wedding took place just two weeks before the liquidation of the ghetto, in June 1944. Mom's attitude was "Time is short and we don't know if we are going to survive, so let's grab some happiness." With his typical tongue-in-cheek humor, my father would tell us that in escaping the ghetto two weeks later, he was running away from Mama. We knew that this was not true, but it became our family joke.

One of the amazing things about my parents was that they both had an incredible sense of humor. They always found a reason to laugh and laughter was part of our home environment; yes, I was blessed! Considering all the traumas they suffered, it is amazing that they were still able to laugh. In fact, my mother stated that humor was one of the traits which kept her and her closest friend, Henny, alive in the concentration camp. She adored Henny for her wonderful sense of humor—and for saving her life.

Yes, friendships were extremely important to Mom. She made sure to tell us about how she and Henny were devoted to each other's survival. After coming to the U.S., Mom and Henny would visit each other often, either in their home in Connecticut or in ours in New York—with the children. Mom always maintained close contact with the other survivor friends from Lithuania, both in the U.S. and in Israel. Our families would meet up for holidays, weekends, summer vacations and special celebrations. The children were included in these events. In addition to large Jewish holidays, the biggest event my parents ever hosted was in 1969, for their 25th wedding anniversary. Of course, they wanted to celebrate their marriage, but they also felt the need to celebrate their survival, their accomplishments and their good fortune—and life—with those who understood from whence they came.

Mama grieved terribly for those she lost. She told us that before leaving Germany to come to the U.S., she went to the site of the Dachau monument to say goodbye to her father's memory. When our grandparents died in Israel, she said: "At least they have a grave where we can mourn." She always lamented the fact that her parents and two sisters had no gravesite for her to visit. Thus, after she moved, once again, to Israel from the U.S. in 1991, she had Papa's body reinterred in a cemetery in Israel, and purchased the adjoining plot for herself. She wanted to establish a place for the family to come together and meet annually in memoriam. While she mourned our papa, she always knew that the years of life after the war were a gift.

My parents did not believe in organized religion or in God. Mom said she stopped believing because of the war. In fact, I remember my mother commenting that she didn't have to fast on Yom Kippur because she had "fasted" enough during the war. Nevertheless, they followed the holiday traditions with all the cultural details. But they did believe in fate, as they retold so many war stories of fate and coincidence. Each of those stories are detailed in her memoir.

Impact Mama always expected us to be happy. In fact, she would get angry or concerned if I did not show happiness. After all, what reason did I have not to be happy? They had had it worse. So, in order to please her, whether I was or I wasn't happy, I had to look happy, as my problems seemed inconsequential.

When our family gets together, from wherever we are in the world, it is always a party, with lots of food, lots of wine and lots of love and laughs. This, by itself, is reason to be happy. While Mom was alive, she was the emotional, cultural and social center of our universe, but we try, regardless of the distances, to remain in touch and updated on all the good and the bad in everyone's life. We talk and write frequently and visit whenever our responsibilities allow. We revel in our growing families of children and grandchildren. Needless to say, the current technology has helped immeasurably, and those blue aerogrammes are now a vague memory from the past.

The bond among the children of the Kovno survivors is very special, despite the fact that many of us did not maintain contact, in some cases for 60 years. Nevertheless, when we have an opportunity to make contact, it is a close relationship based on a shared history. We are each interested, and seemingly take pride, in hearing about each of our accomplishments.

And, indeed, as Mama predicted, our parents' gravesite has become a focal point for our family, for grieving, for memories and, what we have dubbed "the family update." This is when we each write a description of the latest news about our families—and read it aloud at our parents' tombstones. We conduct this unique tradition in order to celebrate our lives and families—in the hope that Mom and Papa are listening. These updates are informative, sensitive and always humorous. We all realize how fortunate we are in having this tradition and this site at which to convene—thanks to Mama.

And our humor is a wonderful trait that we inherited, or learned, from our parents. We always try to frame everything with humor— no matter how difficult. The jokes, the songs and the laughter— sometimes to tears—are something that we share just among us, face to face and even in telephone conversations. And the strong bond we share is envied by others. I can see that my children also have a sense of humor and are strongly bonded, and this makes me happy.

I am very attached to the Jewish and Yiddish culture and history, especially after studying and researching at many opportunities. Nevertheless, I developed a cynical attitude toward organized religion. I am sure this is a direct response to my family's traumatic experiences, grief and losses. However, keeping our heritage and traditions is of great importance to me. As a result of my travels, research and cross-cultural experiences, I studied and learned about many other cultures and their religions. I have come to understand and respect the importance and centrality of religion to most people. I conduct cross-cultural trainings for members of multicultural organizations, for families in transition and as part of university graduate courses. I have also come to realize that in order to truly understand another culture, we must first understand our own.

EDUCATION, HARD WORK AND WORK AS THERAPY

In my mother's mind, and in her philosophy, work was life, work was therapy—and work will keep you alive. Indeed, she described her various jobs in the ghetto and in the concentration camp with a cynical pride, such as cleaning toilets, digging anti-tank ditches or resurfacing the airport runway. The message to us was that no matter how hard the work, even in the frigid winters, you must keep on working to survive. At various times during the ghetto years, she worked doing laundry, darning, ironing and sewing. While she might have learned basic sewing at home, it was here that she developed her sewing skills that helped the family economy in the U.S. She taught us her motto "You must always say you can do it, even if you can't; you can always figure out how to do it afterwards." She made sure to tell us about jobs she took, even though she did not know how to do it. She told us about how she, herself, registered her mother and sisters upon their arrival in the concentration camp, because she stepped forward to be a registrar just a day prior.

Mom was what we would call today - a workaholic. Her famous admonition at home was "*zitz nit mit kayn laydike hendt*" (don't sit with idle hands). She was the original multi-tasker before it became fashionable. As a teenager, perhaps I resented it; she was always busy and never wasted time. If she was watching TV she would also do handwork, alterations, ironing; she could never sit without "doing" something. She would never complain, never ask for help and never, ever, rest. It happened rarely, but as a kid, if I ever saw my mother lie down during the day, I knew she was ill or in pain. Imagine, after all these years, that I still recall when my mother returned from one of her dental surgeries and I found her lying on the couch in the middle of the day; I became duly worried. Relaxation, for Mama, was non-existent.

Another one of Mom's mantras was, "*azay vi men bet zich ous, azay shloft men*" (the way one makes one's bed, that's the way one sleeps). To us, this meant that you will get what you deserve if you do not work hard enough and prepare, i.e. "Don't be lazy!" She could never tolerate laziness, lack of preparation, organization, or lack of responsibility.

She also believed in work therapy. She did not believe in the need for psychologists or psychiatrists, in fact, she derided those who sought out such therapy. Mom always said: "We are not crazy, so we don't go to psychiatrists." Her solution for all life's problems was work therapy. Ironically, her greatest fear was to lose her mental capacity. She used to say: "If I become mentally incapable, shoot me." Sadly, this is exactly how she spent her last years, with dementia. She couldn't do any of her work therapy—and we couldn't do anything to help her fulfill her wish.

And, of course, Mom taught us the importance of education, above all. To her, education is key, because no one can take away what is in your mind. She often mentioned her dream to study and become a doctor. But, of course, her high school education and her dream were violently interrupted at 16. She told us that the war was an excellent education. We all laughed when her good friend would quip: "Yeh [sic], I am a Bergen-Belsen graduate."

Impact I recall one summer when I went through what I call a "funk," which might be called "depression" today. So what did

Mom do? She absolutely did not believe in psychologists, so she ran out and bought me rug-hooking kits and I completed three rugs that summer. Another time, after leaving home for university, I was very homesick and called my mother on the phone. She instructed me to take everything out of my drawers and closet, clean it out, iron the items, fold them carefully and rearrange my closet. To this day, when I am upset, angry, sad, or nostalgic, I delve into a "work" project until the difficult emotions dissipate.

For us, higher education was an expectation, and my sisters and I all graduated from universities—so did my children. Later in life, I eventually achieved a doctoral degree. I joked with Mom and my sisters, saying: "So now Mom has a doctor in the family; well, maybe not *that* kind of a doctor, but a doctor nonetheless." I was so glad that my mother was alive and still healthy to celebrate this event; I know it made her so happy and proud to be in the audience.

All three of Mom's daughters were deeply influenced by her; we are all workaholics, never rest, are not lazy and rarely complain. To this day, I cannot watch TV without doing additional work, like ironing, reading, answering emails, cooking, etc. I cannot even sit and rest during a vacation without having a reading or writing project to do. And we are each hard working, responsible, and outstanding organizers and planners—and so are my children.

FINANCIAL SECURITY AND FRUGALITY

Both my parents came from families that were financially comfortable before the war—never very rich, but never hungry. But, needless to say, one year under the Soviets, four years under the Nazis and five years reunifying the family and living in the DP camps after liberation, and the first six or so years in the U.S., took a toll. As new immigrants to the U.S., we were very poor. We lived in one of the poorest neighborhoods in Brooklyn, as this was all my parents could afford in the early years.

Stories of having only enough money to purchase one lamb chop per day—only for their child—pervaded my childhood. I remember eating in a restaurant for the first time when I was a teenager. Needless to say, we never ever wasted food or threw out leftovers; they were finished down to the last bite, or "repurposed" in a new recipe. My father's stories of hunger and eating raw eggs stolen from a chicken coop shocked us and left a strong impression. He embellished the story by saying: "I popped a hole in it and sucked out the raw interior."

In later years, the refrigerator was always full of food. Nevertheless, we always ate what was prepared and put on the table; no one could opt out or demand something different. This was the way it was. We, kids, clearly understood that this was a non-negotiable; finicky eaters? Not in my mother's house!

My mother would never, ever entertain the idea of leaving her children with anyone in order to go out to work. Thus, it was up to my father to bring some financial security to the family. However, his immigrant income was only enough for subsistence living in the early years before they became citizens. In the later years, when we were older, she began supplementing the household income by doing alterations at home, as she became a skilled seamstress under the tutelage of my grandmother.

Due to my mother's seamstress skills, and her careful and frugal economics, she always managed to put aside some monies for the proverbial "rainy day." There were numerous rainy days, but the big one came at the end of 1969, when my father, along with tens of thousands of engineers around the U.S. were laid off after the end of the NASA lunar mission—all on the same day. All these high level engineers were accepting even menial jobs to support their families. Many lost their homes because they could not continue paying their mortgages. However, my mother had squirreled away money which allowed them to pay the mortgage while my father found part time work. She saved our home! She was a survivor.

As a widowed senior, after immigrating back to Israel, she lived off her savings, some German reparation payments, and Social Security. She saved and saved and saved ... and shocked us all when we learned that she had the funds to afford relocating to a senior home in Israel.

Impact I started working very young, at around eleven years old, as a babysitter, a job I continued to do throughout the time I lived in my parents' home. While in high school and college, I also worked in a real estate office as an office manager. I saved considerable sums of money and felt proud that I could pay my own expenses; I also felt that supporting myself would be helpful to the family. I never asked them for any money—ever!

After marriage, in a constant effort to maintain our household economics and ensure that we could live within our means, I rarely hired anyone to do what I could do myself, i.e. house cleaning, laundry, ironing, gardening, babysitting, etc. I proudly considered these actions a demonstration of my ability to survive. I was proud of my skills, whether buying on sale, only purchasing produce in season, buying-selling in second-hand shops, saving wrappings, bags, silver foil, containers, etc. In the past it was derided as "frugality" or "being cheap." Today, it is commended as fiscal responsibility, recycling and environmental awareness—higher virtues. I never apologized for this frugality, rather, I considered it a demonstration of strength. I managed my household expenses carefully, as living in Israel was always a financial struggle. We never had an overdraft in the bank, as is very common in Israel. All this did change somewhat, as our economic possibilities increased years later.

I still fight my own internal battle before throwing out bread with signs of mold—or any leftovers in the fridge. I am skilled at cooking a meal with whatever is in the fridge. Even with a prescribed recipe, I always modify it to "use up" whatever is available under the mantra of "waste not, want not." In addition, my children always ate whatever was put on the table. There was no negotiation about the menu, nor about unhealthy and unnecessary snacks in the home. However, today, my adult children have an aversion to leftovers. They joke about the home economics of their youth, and I bristle at the waste of their adulthood.

As an educator and educational leader, I have had to deal with innumerable families, each with a wide array of behaviors—some admirable and others questionable. It has given me a wide perspective on functional and dysfunctional families. With the luxury of hindsight, professional experience and advancing age, I am able to look at my own parents and my upbringing with different eyes. Just after I became a mother, I began to view my own parents with awe, especially my mother. The ability to not only survive horrors, but to thrive, to be able to overcome insurmountable challenges, both as a grief-stricken survivor, refugee and immigrant, are certainly worthy of admiration. And, to give love, maintain optimism and humor throughout—that is worthy of accolades. Most of their odd behaviors and idiosyncrasies have either been forgotten, forgiven, or have now become the butt of our family jokes. I am unsure if their impact on me was due to nature or to nurture, war or immigration, but, I imagine that it was a combination of them all. In the final analysis, I feel blessed to have been raised by two functional, loving, resilient and devoted human beings, who were my life models.

On my car radio, at the time of writing, I heard the haunting Crosby, Stills, and Nash song, *Teach Your Children*. I found myself in tears while driving and listening to the lyrics which so resonated at this moment of senior introspection. My parents' hell and fears taught me well—their code and their dreams served me well. When they told me of their past, there were many tears. I know that my parents fulfilled their dreams of having a family; I know that they loved me and I hope I gave them happiness and pride. And I hope my children will sing the same.

THE PURPOSE OF THIS BOOK

The purpose of this book has been to memorialize, record, document and preserve this story for current and future generations. In addition, this auto/biography is targeted at various reader groups:

1. Family, friends and Second/Third Generation cohorts: to ensure that they become familiar with and grieve for their past ancestry, so that they can understand and analyze their present identity.

2. Historians and researchers: to add more detail to the body of knowledge with first-hand accounts of survivors and their descendants.

3. Students in educational institutions: to enliven history with personal accounts, develop civic awareness, responsibility and empathy, inspire individual family research, and highlight the results of organized and legalized hate crimes and genocide.

4. Holocaust deniers and hate groups: to add testimonies and documentation to counter conspiracy theories, lies, evil motives and nefarious agendas.

Every person who has lived for any length of time has a story that could fill a book. The longer their lives, the longer the tables of contents. Typically, each life story is shared with those nearest and dearest. However, when lives are cut short in the most brutal and unexpected manner, such as during this period of genocide, when young and old were quickly whisked away, hidden, or massacred, and when all continuity and knowledge about their lives vanished in an instant, these stories become fractured, open ended and disappear into unknown graves, or into smoke. Those who survived the horrors, and those who worried from far away, may or may not know about the fate of those who disappeared or were murdered; they were robbed of all information about their families and friends. How cruel and painful not to have the knowledge, nor a gravesite, field or cemetery to visit.

If Holocaust stories are not recorded, written and made available to the public they will disappear into dust and ashes—just like the millions. That would be a repeat of the genocide. I hope that by writing this book, readers will have an opportunity for review, remembrance, reflection and truth.

BIBLIOGRAPHY

Ancestry Memorial Pages (nd). Kovno Ghetto Partisans and Chaim Yellin Stories, https://www.fold3.com/page/286123943-the-kovno-ghetto-partisans-chaim-yelin/stories, fold3 by ancestry.

Aronson, H. (1994). "Oral History Project," U.S. Holocaust Memorial Museum, https://www.ushmm.org/exhibition/personal-history/media_oi.php?MediaId=2609

Aronson, H. (2009). "Oral History Project," U.S. Holocaust Memorial Museum, https://www.ushmm.org/exhibition/personal-history/media_oi.php?MediaId=2869

Baack, G.A. (2016). *The Inheritors: Moving Forward from Generational Trauma,* She Writes Press, California.

Baran, R. (1990). "Oral History Project," U.S. Holocaust Memorial Museum.

https://collections.ushmm.org/search/catalog/vha36618

Baran, R. (2017). Telephone interviews with Ettie Zilber.

Beasley, N.W. (2015). *Izzy's Fire: Finding Humanity in the Holocaust,* Posie Press, Virginia.

Blackman Slivka, R. "Oral History Project," U.S. Holocaust Memorial Museum. https://www.ushmm.org/wlc/en/media_oi.php?MediaId=1202&ModuleId=10005197

Bottner, T. (2017). *Among the Reeds: The true story of how a family survived the Holocaust*, Amsterdam Publishers, The Netherlands.

CBC Canada (1982). "Extradition of Helmut Rauca for trial in West Germany." http://www.cbc.ca/player/play/1764256990

Dachau Concentration Camp Memorial Archives, (2016). Prisoner Jakob Santockis' arrival, registration and death certificate, Bavarian Foundation.

Desbois, P. (2008). *The Holocaust by Bullets: A Priest's Journey to Uncover the Truth Behind the Murder of 1.5 Million Jews*, St. Martin Press, New York.

Desbois, P. (2018). *In Broad Daylight: The Secret Procedures Behind the Holocaust by Bullets*, Arcade Publishers, New York.

Drywa, D. (2004). *The Extermination of Jews in Stutthof Concentration Camp 1939-1945*, Stutthof Museum in Sztutowo, Gdansk.

Elkes, J. (1997). *Dr. Elkhanan Elkes of the Kovno Ghetto*, Paraclete Press, Massachusetts.

Epstein, H. (1979). *Children of the Holocaust*, G.P. Putnam's Sons, New York.

Faitelson, A. (1998). *The Escape from the IXth Fort, Kaunas, Lithuania*, Gefen Publishing House Ltd, Spausdino "Gabijos" and Jerusalem.

Gabis, R. (2015). *A Guest at the Shooters' Banquet*, Bloomsbury, New York.

Galperin Godin, N. (1989). "Oral History Project," U.S. Holocaust Memorial Museum. https://collections.ushmm.org/search/catalog/irn504575

Gar, J. (1948). *The Extermination of the Jews of Kovno*, Steven Spielberg

Digital Yiddish Library, No. 00549, National Yiddish Book Center, Mass. https://www.yiddishbookcenter.org/collections/yiddish-books/spb-nybc200549/gar-joseph-umkum-fun-der-yidisher-kovne

Gempel, B. (1983). Video testimonial delivered at the University of British Columbia, Canada.

Gens, Ada Ustjanauskas (2008). "Oral History Project," U.S. Holocaust Memorial Museum. https://collections.ushmm.org/search/catalog/irn36962

Gilbert, M. (1982). *Atlas of the Holocaust*, Michael Joseph Ltd., London.

Gilbert, M. (1985). *The Holocaust: A history of the Jews of Europe during the Second World War*, Henry Holt & Company, New York.

Haas, A. (1990). *In the Shadow of the Holocaust*, Cornell University Press, New York.

HEART: Holocaust Education and Archive Research Team. http://www.holocaustresearchproject.org/othercamps/stutthof.html

Holocaust Atlas of Lithuania, "VII Fort Massacres."

http://www.holocaustatlas.lt/EN/#a_atlas/search/bendri=VII%20Fort.vietove=.aukos=.from_year=0.from_month=0.from_day=.to_year=0.to_month=0.to_day=.killers=/page/1/item/23/

Kaunas Archives, (1931). Floor Plans of Kapsu Gatwe 33.

Kellerman, N.P. (2013). "Epigenetic transmission of Holocaust trauma: can nightmares be inherited?" *Israel Journal of Psychiatry and Related Sciences*, 50 (1), pp. 33-9.

Levin, D. (2000). *The Litvaks: A Short History of the Jews in Lithuania*. Yad Vashem Press, Jerusalem.

Lewis, H. (1998). "Oral History Project," U.S. Holocaust Memorial Museum. https://collections.ushmm.org/search/catalog/vha47708

Littman, S. (1993). *War Criminal on Trial: Rauca of Kaunas*, Key Porter Books, Toronto.

Loughlin, B. (2005). "WW2: People's War," gathered by the BBC. http://www.bbc.co.uk/history/ww2peopleswar/stories/01/a8099201.shtml

Lurie, E. (1958). *A Living Witness – Kovno Ghetto*. Dvir Publ., Tel Aviv.

Meisel, J. "Oral History Project," U.S. Holocaust Memorial Museum. https://www.ushmm.org/wlc/en/media_oi.php?ModuleId=10005197&MediaId=1156

Mishell, W.W. (1998). *Kaddish for Kovno*, Chicago Review Press, Inc., Chicago.

Oshry, E. (1995). *The Annihilation of Lithuanian Jewry*, Judaica Press, Inc., New York.

Petrikenas, V. & Kosas, M. (2011). *VII Fortas: Lietuviska Tragedija: The History of the First Concentration Camp in Lithuania*, Arx Reklama, Kaunas.

Rapoport, S. (2016). *A Pedigreed Jew: Between There and Here-Kovno and Israel*, Amberley Publishing, U.K.

Rassen, J. (2007). "We want to live," published by the family of J. Rassen. http://www.jewishgen.org/yizkor/WantToLive/WantToLive.html

Rodriguez, T. (2015). "Descendants of Holocaust survivors have altered stress hormones," *Scientific American*, https://www.scientificamerican.com/article/descendants-of-holocaust-survivors-have-altered-stress-hormones/

Sidrer, Liova (1987). Interview with Ettie Zilber.

Sidrer, Lottie (2010). Interview & presentation at Living History Day, WBAIS International School.

https://sites.google.com/a/wbais.net/living-history-2010/home/lotte-sidrer

Sidrer, Zlata (1979, 1987). Interviews with Ettie Zilber.

State Museum Stutthof in Sztutowo (1999). Certificate verifying imprisonment in Stutthof Concentration Camp.

Tory, A. (1990). *Surviving the Holocaust: The Kovno Ghetto Diary*, Harvard University Press, Cambridge, Mass.

U.S. Holocaust Memorial Museum (USHMM, 1997). *The Hidden History of the Kovno Ghetto: Project of the U.S. Holocaust Memorial Council*, Little, Brown and Company, Washington, DC.

U.S. Holocaust Memorial Museum (USHMM, nd). *Stutthof,* https://encyclopedia.ushmm.org/content/en/article/stutthof

Virginia Holocaust Museum. http://www.va-holocaust.com/

Walworth Barbour American International School - WBAIS (2010, 2011). Living History Project.

World of ORT (2010). "ORT and the Displaced Persons Camps." https://dpcamps.ort.org/camps/germany/us-zone/us-zone-v/

Yad Vashem. Research Projects. http://www.yadvashem.org/yv/en/about/institute/killing_sites_catalog_details_full.asp?region=Kaunas&title=Kaunas%20county

Yahad in Unum Organization. http://www.yahadinunum.org/

Zilber, E. (2009). *Third Culture Kids: Children of International School Educators*, U.K., John Catt, Ltd., www.ettiezilber.com/books

Zilber, E. (2017). *Catalysts for a Career in InternationalSchools*, ECIS InFocus, https://www.ettiezilber.com/publication-1/

Zilber, E. (2017, November). *The Story of Jewish Volunteer Jakubas Santockis*, Litvaks organization, http://www.litvaks.org/projects/the-ruvin-bun-award/jewish-volunteer-jakubas-santockis/

PHOTOS

*Santocki family in Adutiskis/Haydutishok, Svencionys,
Lithuania. 1932. Visiting grandparents Standing left: Eta Zivov
Santocki; Right: Yakov Santockis; Seated left: grandmother
Ester Liba Disner Zivov; on lap Ida: middle: Zlata; Seated
right: grandfather Zalman Gershon Zivov; on lap-Nechama.*

*Santocki family, Kaunas, 1934. Left to right: grandmother
Ester Liba Disner Zivov holding baby Genya b. 1933 named
after Grandfather Zalman Gershon; Standing: Zlata, mother
Eta, Ida; Seated: father Yakov, Nechama.*

*Santocki sisters, Kaunas, 1937. Left to right: Ida, Genya (on stool),
Zlata, Nechama.*

Santocki family, Kaunas, 1940. Last photo taken before the German invasion. Standing left to right: Ida, Nechama, Zlata; Seated left: Eta, center Genya, Right: Yakov.

Liova Sidrer, Kaunas, 1925. The SS demanded to know where this child was during the children's Aktsia in 1944. The parents pointed to 21-year-old Liova, who was sitting in the room.

Sidrer family, Kaunas, 1931. Seated: father Feival Sidrer, Reva on lap; Standing: Liova, mother Chaya Kamionski Sidrer; family miraculously survived the horrors individually.

Post Office, Laisves Aleja, Kaunas. Electrical work was done by my grandfather, Feivalis Sidreris; plaque in front lobby recognizing his work.

Laisves Aleja, Kaunas. Pedestrian "Freedom boulevard"; Zlata's favorite street.

Poshkosh Gatwe #14, Kaunas. Sidrer home until 1933. Street entrance/courtyard.

Sports clothing factory, Viliampole. Feival Sidrer constructed this building as a metal foundry with their home upstairs. Confiscated by the Soviets, 1940.

Kalnyechu Gatwe #15, Zaliakalnis, Kaunas. Sidrers lived here from 1940-1941 during Russian occupation, German occupation and forced relocation to ghetto.

Kapsu Gatwe #33 changed to #59, Kaunas. Possibly Santocki home & butcher shop until August, 1941 after forced relocation to Kovno Ghetto.

186

Seventh Fort, Kaunas. Site of massacre of 5000 men and boys, July, 1941. Santocki family imprisoned; Yakov Santockis was spared at the last moment.

Savanoris Medal given to military volunteers of War of Independence. Given to Yakov Santockis by President of Lithuania; it saved his life at the Seventh Fort massacres July, 1941.

Kovno Ghetto, 1941-44. Feival Sidrer, (left) at the Ghetto sawmill. Published with permission of the Lithuanian Central State Archives, Vilnius, p. 144, USHMM Hidden History of Kovno Ghetto.

Kovno Ghetto to Ninth Fort, October 29, 1941, the Big Aktsia (roundup). Jewish prisoners marching to their deaths; drawing by Feival Sidrer in 1948.

Ninth Fort, Viliampole. Monument at the killing fields.

Nation's House Cultural Center, Kaunas. Building requisitioned as Gestapo headquarters 1941-45.

Kovno Ghetto, Slabodka/ Viliampole. Typical ghetto houses.

Stutthof Concentration Camp, Sztutowo, Poland. Front gate.

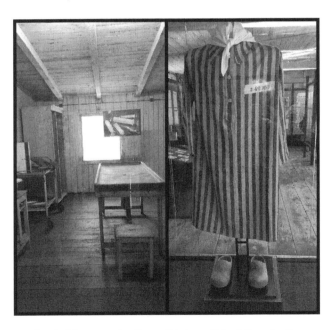

Stutthof Concentration Camp, Sztutowo, Poland. Examination table, uniform, clogs.

Stutthof Museum Archive, July, 1944. Zlata Santocki's registration #41410.

Birkenau Concentration Camp, Oświęcim, Poland. Entrance and monument to those murdered; pool where ashes from crematoria were dumped.

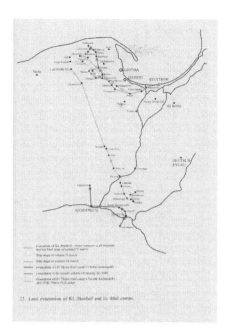

*Map of "Evacuation Routes" death march routes, Jan-March, 1945.
Reprinted with permission of Danuta Drywa.*

Road sign along death march, Poland. The Stutthof Victims'
Road.

Poland. One of the many barns along the death march. Did Mama sleep here?

Luzino, Poland. Church along death march, with mural to the Evacuation/death march; Zlata possibly slept here.

Proust/Pruscz, Poland. Mama slaved here on February 5, 1945, her 20th birthday.

Wejherowo, Poland. Prison where Zlata's column of women prisoners slept, Feb-March, 1945.

Gdinya, Poland, 1945. After liberation. Zlata left of Feival with black hair covering; Henny right of Feival with white hair covering.

Lodz, Poland, 1946. After liberation. Seated: Feival Sidrer, Chaya Sidrer. Standing: Reva Sidrer, Nechama Santocki.

DP camp Landsberg am Lech, Germany, c. 1947. Camp hospital staff, Zlata (top-middle).

DP camp Landsberg am Lech, Germany, 1948. Feival and Chaya Sidrer listening to the radio during UN vote on the independence of Israel.

*Landsberg am Lech, Germany, 2007. Hospital where I was
born in 1949.*

*DP camp Landsberg am Lech, Germany, 1949. Zlata and Baby
Eta/Ettie.*

En route to the USA, May, 1950. Zlata and Ettie onboard SS General Baloo.

Plainview, New York 1968. Zlata and the girls. Left to right: Zlata (now Lottie in the USA), Ettie Sidrer, Edit Shneorson, Jeanne Sidrer, Nechama Shneorson (Zlata's surviving sister), Rena Sidrer.

*Tel Aviv, Israel, 1995. Zlata gives speech to Lithuanian Association
- 50 years since liberation.*

*Miami, Florida, 2008. The last meeting of Zlata and Henny, soul
sisters.*

Miami, Florida, 2008. Mama and her girls. Bottom to top:
Zlata, Rena, Ettie, Jeanne.

Israel, 2010 & 2011. Zlata telling her story to High School
students; reprinted with permission of the WBAIS, Israel,
Living History Day.

New York, 2010. Zlata's farewell visit to sister, Nechama Shneorson.

Kadima Israel, 2010. Zlata's 85th birthday.

Kadima, Israel, 2013. Zlata, "Da Shayne Bobe" (the beautiful grandmother) and her 8 grandchildren. Left to right: Adam Zilber, Lee Rabin, Eden Rabin, Dana Zilber, Neri Zilber, Ariel Itzhaky, Ella Itzhaky, Alon Itzhaky.

New York, 2018. Zlata's great grandchildren from Ettie's family: Left to right standing Justin, Adam, Astrid; seated left to right Dana, holding Jack, Yakov, holding Ava, Ettie, holding newest addition – Zoe – named after Zlata. Missing from photo is Neri.

Israel, 2018. Zlata's great grandchildren from Jeanne's family: Tomi and Kai.

Herziliya, Israel, 2017. Zlata and Liova (Lottie & Lou) Sidrer- final resting place – together always.

FURTHER READING

Amsterdam Publishers specializes in memoirs written by Holocaust survivors and their children. Holocaust survivor stories need to be kept alive, especially in today's society. In case you enjoyed reading these memoirs you might be interested in reading other Holocaust memoirs. If you click on any of the book covers you will be directed to the publishers website.

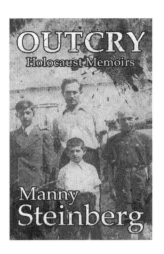

Outcry - Holocaust Memoirs by Manny Steinberg is available as
paperback (ISBN 9789082103137) and eBook. Also published in
French, German, Italian, Chinese and Czech.

Manny Steinberg (1925-2015) spent his teens in Nazi concentration camps in Germany, miraculously surviving while millions perished. This is his story. Born in the Jewish ghetto in Radom (Poland), Steinberg noticed that people of Jewish faith were increasingly being regarded as outsiders. In September 1939 the Nazis invaded, and the nightmare started. The city's Jewish population had no chance of escaping and was faced with starvation, torture, sexual abuse and ultimately deportation.

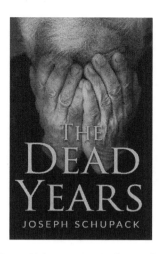

The Dead Years - Holocaust Memoirs by Joseph Schupack is available as paperback (ISBN: 9789492371164) and eBook. German: Tote Jahre.

In *The Dead Years,* Joseph Schupack (1922- 1989) describes his life in Radzyn-Podlaski, a typical Polish shtetl from where he was transported to the concentration camps of Treblinka, Majdanek, Auschwitz, Dora / Nordhausen and Bergen-Belsen during the Second World War. We witness how he struggled to remain true to his own standards of decency and being human. Considering the premeditated and systematic humiliation and brutality, it is a miracle that he survived and came to terms with his memories.

The Dead Years is different from most Holocaust survivor stories. Not only is it a testimony of the 1930s in Poland and life in the Nazi concentration camps - it also serves as a witness statement. This Holocaust book contains a wealth of information, including the names of people and places, for researchers and those interested in WW2, or coming from Radzyn-Podlaski and surroundings. The book takes us through Joseph Schupack's pre-war days, his work in the underground movement, and the murder of his parents, brothers, sister and friends.

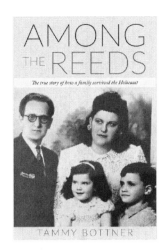

Among the Reeds: The true Story of how a Family survived the Holocaust by Tammy Bottner is available as paperback (ISBN 9789492371287) and eBook.

Watching friends and neighbors arrested for the simple crime of being Jewish, a young couple in Belgium face impossible decisions during WW2. Should they send their two-year-old son into hiding without them? Would that save his life? And what about their newborn daughter?

In this moving family memoir, the author, the daughter of that little boy, recounts the astounding courage that led to her family's survival during the Holocaust. In spite of numerous near-misses, the family not only made it through the war, but were reunited when the Nazis were defeated.

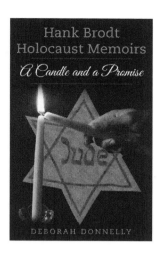

Hank Brodt Holocaust Memoirs – A Candle and a Promise is available as paperback (ISBN 9781537653488) and eBook.

A story of resilience, *Hank Brodt Holocaust Memoirs - A Candle and a Promise* makes the memories of Holocaust survivor Hank Brodt come alive. It offers a detailed historical account of being a Jewish teenager under the Nazi regime, shedding light on sickening truths in an honest, matter-of-fact way.

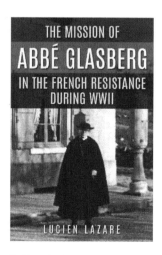

The Mission of Abbé Glasberg in the French Resistance during WWII by Lucien Lazare is available as paperback (ISBN 9781522840954) and eBook.

The Mission of Abbé Glasberg is the fascinating story of a priest - of Jewish origins - who dedicated himself to the task of helping the refugees who were streaming into France during the years preceding World War II. Together with Father Chaillet, Abbé Glasberg created the ecumenical Amitié Chrétienne in May 1942 with the full support of Cardinal Gerlier, archbishop of Lyon.

Salo Muller

See You Tonight
And Promise to Be a Good Boy!
War Memories

See You Tonight and Promise to be a Good Boy! War memories by Salo Muller is available as paperback (ISBN 9789492371553) and eBook.

'See you tonight, and promise to be a good boy!' were the last words his mother said to Salo Muller in 1942 when she took him to school in Amsterdam, right before she was deported to Auschwitz. She and her husband were arrested a few hours later and taken to Westerbork, from where they would later board the train that took them to Auschwitz.

The book is, in his own words, "the story of a little boy who experienced the most horrible things, but got through it somehow and ended up in a great place." Salo, at only 5 years old, spent his time during the Second World War in hiding, in as much as eight different locations in the Netherlands. The book tells the story of his experiences during ww2, but also explains how he tried to make sense of his life after the war, being a young orphan.

Holocaust Memoirs of a Bergen-Belsen Survivor & Classmate of Anne Frank by Nanette Blitz Konig is available as paperback (ISBN 9789492371614) and eBook.

In these compelling and award-winning Holocaust memoirs, Nanette Blitz Konig relates her amazing story of survival during WW2 when she, together with her family and millions of other Jews were imprisoned by the Nazi's with a minimum chance of survival. Nanette (b. 1929) was a class mate of Anne Frank in the Jewish Lyceum of Amsterdam. They met again in the Bergen-Belsen concentration camp shortly before Anne died.

Rescued from the Ashes. The Diary of Leokadia Schmidt, Survivor of the Warsaw Ghetto is available as paperback (ISBN 9789493056060) and eBook.

The diary of a young Jewish housewife who, together with her husband and five-month-old baby, fled the Warsaw ghetto at the last possible moment and survived the Holocaust hidden on the "Aryan" side of town in the loft of a run-down tinsmith's shed.

Remembering Ravensbrück - Holocaust to Healing by Natalie B. Hess is available as paperback (ISBN: 9789493056237) and as Kindle eBook.

In her luminous and engrossing memoir, Natalie B. Hess takes us from a sheltered childhood in a small town in Poland into the horrors of the Holocaust.

When her parents are rounded up and perish in the Treblinka concentration camp, a Gentile family temporarily hides six-year-old Natalia. Later, protected by a family friend, she is imprisoned in her city's ghetto, before she is sent to a forced-labor camp, and finally, Ravensbrück Concentration camp, from which, at nine, she is liberated.

Hess's compelling portrait in which terror is muted by gratitude and gentle humor, shares the story of so many immigrants dislocated by tyranny and war. Through her experience as a child separated from her parents, a teenager, young woman, wife, mother, college professor, and later a widow, Hess shows the power of the human spirit to survive and thrive.

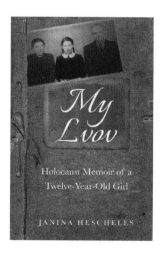

My Lvov. A Holocaust memoir of a twelve-year-old girl by Janina Hescheles

While still twelve years old, Janina Hescheles (b. 1931) wrote this harrowing report from her hiding place in Cracow. The notebook, filled with clear childlike writing, was fortunately preserved. She tells about the German occupation of Lvov, the loss of her parents, about the Ghetto and mass murder in the notorious forced-labor camp Janowska in Lvov. Thrown into the abyss of horror, Janina understood and sensed more than could be expected of someone her age.

Printed in Great Britain
by Amazon

75785980R00127